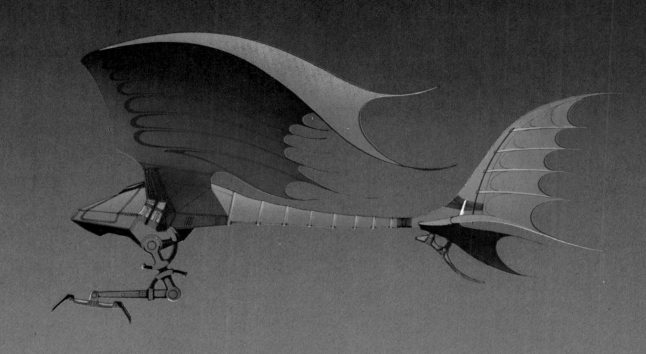

Roger Dean

Views

By arrangement with
Dragon's World Ltd.
Limpsfield
Surrey RH8 0DY
Great Britain

Produced and designed by Roger Dean.

Line photography processed by TANTRUMS.

Printed and Bound in Singapore by APA Press

Text by Dominy Hamilton and Carla Capalbo in association with Roger Dean.
With an introduction to the text and to the architectural section by Donald Lehmkuhl

CONTENTS

Introduction by Donald Lehmkuhl   7
Some notes on Roger Dean's technique   9
Furniture   13
Record Covers   24
YES   97
"Retreat Pod"   129
Architecture   132
List of principal pictures   155

Acknowledgments

I would particularly like to express my thanks to Donald Lehmkuhl for the care and patience he gave to this project, and to Dominy and Carla for their forbearance and long hours spent compiling the text. The proofing of the colour plates was of an exceptionally high quality, and for maintaining this standard I would like to thank Alan Jeffries, Ian Hamilton, and all at Mansell Litho. For his work and help at the eleventh hour in the publishing of this book I would like to thank Hubert Schaafsma, and also in this connection Jenne Caserotto, Jenny Jacobs, and Al for their good advice. Finally, for their support and encouragement in my work generally I would like to thank Bill and Jane,

Donald Lehmkuhl

Dominy Hamilton was born on the 22nd of November, 1949, in London. After dropping out of the sixth form at 17 she had a succession of jobs in London, but after a few years she returned to her studies. Since 1971 she has been studying History and Theory of Art at the University of Sussex, and she graduated in the summer of 1975. She plans to continue her studies at postgraduate level.

Thank you for everything to Terry O'Reilly, Richard Hamilton, Rita Donagh, Pauletta and Nanna.

Dominy Hamilton

Carla Capalbo was born in New York City in 1952, and has lived and studied in England since 1961. She majored in the History and Theory of Art at Sussex University. Currently she is studying art in London and working on a pasta cookbook.

Donald Lehmkuhl

INTRODUCTION

When you look at the work of Roger Dean, you may come away with the feeling that you have been told a truth. (Truthfulness is, perhaps, Dean's proper signature, his fingerprints—individual, invisible, there.) Yet what is this truth you have been told? It is not about "received" reality. Dean does not say "see this canned air. You have never seen canned air before." He could do this if he wanted to. No. He shows us insects with nuclear power, fish swimming in air, waterfalls without a source. He fuses Stonehenge with spacecraft and gives elephants wings. He goes out of this world. Out of received reality. He pursues the incomparable. Where he goes, is also reality. His work is about this reality: about the true nature of things, of forms, of appearances, of feelings, spiritual feelings, feelings which (like music) are themselves both perceptions and stirred memories of places, events, creations long ago, or—more likely— long ahead. But the impression Dean powerfully conveys is Now. For this reality is everywhere. Obviously this reality will not be found by sleep-walking through the steel and glass asylum we call Metropolis. One must be awake, aware, to see it. Roger Dean conjures this awareness. Seer-surgeon, he strips away the spiritual caul that lets pass only the light of automatic reality. He transmutes eyesight into vision, confounding allusion and illusion and elusion to a point of trembling mystery. To the naked eye he lays bare the heart of the matter. Matter, the deceiver. Matter, the conceiver. "I'm not painting a picture," Dean says. "I'm not being mystical. I'm not being profound. I'm not being exclusive. I'm just seeing the basic thing there is to be seen. I'm not hiding behind an aura. I'm putting down what everybody can see if they want to."

Dean's work is about the mind in matter, about the unaccountability of form, about the visible invisibility of energy, about the inscrutability of space. About evolution. About perception. About the relationship of subject to object. Everything he depicts, everything he designs, almost everything he touches, slightly alters, emerges with a peculiar, significant look. The look of *objectness*. Dean insists that everything we surround ourselves with should have this look, this smile or frown of authority, of essence, of exactness, of allness: of the essential. A tiger should be all tigers as well as all tiger, a locomotive all locomotion. Every object should have its objectness, be its objectness. "The role of the person who's struggling to create things, who's thinking of himself as someone who's creating something that doesn't yet exist, is to catch and convey the essence of his creation," says Dean. Creation creates its creator, creates the essential. Dean attempts to instill objectness into everything he inspires with reality: a badger, an insect-spaceship, a tree, a cave, a fish, a lizard, an ogre, an orchid, a house.

Dean is not a painter, an illustrator, a fabricator, an artist. He is, rather, two things: a describer and a creator. His drawing ability is secondary, a tool in the hands of an explorer who renders on paper what he sees or what he intends to see. Dean, for instance, is fond of modifying the classic *objet trouvé*—whether conventional driftwood, a plastic elephant, a bird's skull, an abandoned wardrobe—into something that is both old and new, something that looks like the whole of evolution out of a transistorized future. Dean is busy manufacturing an alternative reality that is strange-familiar, fantastic-real. It is that world which counts, as far as Dean is concerned, and not his interpretations of it. Dean rejects dream scenes. His preference is for the three-dimensional, for the materialization outside him of what he sees inside him. And so he designs his own chairs, his own beds, his own fire-places, his own walls and floors. His own house.

What must be immediately understood about Roger Dean, then, is that his range and intentions extend far beyond the astonishing record cover designs that have brought him public notice. His principal concern, in fact, is with architecture, both domestic and urban and, by extension, with city planning and planned civilizations.

Take another look at Dean's record cover designs and seek out in them all the dwelling places, all the habitations: the houses and lighthouses, the villages and cities, the caves and castles. In them you will see Roger Dean's vision of an architecture that possesses objectness. This architecture seems to have grown from the earth, seems to have been there forever, seems also to have followed the curving spaces of man's mind. These are not glowing illuminations like the decorations in a medieval manuscript. They are serious designs that Dean would like to see made real and lived in.

That he would truly like to see all these forms brought into,material reality is shown by the fastidious model he has built of his house. This house is unique. It burgeons from the earth. It sprouts. It flowers. It clusters. Now it's a hive. Now a clump of grapes. Now a clutch of eggs. Now a growth of coral. Now of crystals. It is all of these things. It is none of these things. Because it is itself, and only and always a house. Strange. Yes. Strangely familiar. Strangely natural. Strangely correct. And friendly, very friendly. At first glance, its concentration of form appears assymetrical, the eye roves everywhere unconfined by the restraint of angles. Further glances reveal not forms but form, mathematically perfect, embodying a centre as secret and mysterious as the whorl of a seashell. This house is objectness. Dean's

ambition is to build an entire world around him, around us all, founded on objectness. He invites his viewer to participate with him in this world, to find in it something the viewer already knows, already recognizes as if he had seen it before in a time-space warp. To this extent, then, Roger Dean's pictorial visions are propaganda for a psycho-emotional philosophy of the human being. He is not saying "back to Nature." Rather, "we go forward *through* Nature." It is this very propaganda that provokes from all his drawings the impression that these places, these creatures are alive and well and living somewhere we could visit—if we only had the right ticket or the right map.

The vision is the thing for Roger Dean. Like all visionaries, Dean is a loner. He is no part of a movement or school. He has no direct antecedents. The suggestion that his work is surrealist is inaccurate, misleading, for he is not trying to confuse or compound identities, he is not trying to mine the ego or undermine the id. He is trying to define entities, and everything he does is work in progress of definition. Moreover, every dragon from his hand, every helicopter, every house, every flower, is related. They are all descriptions from The Other Reality. Bound together, they form one large picture. Looking at this book should be a voyage deep-in and far-out, a trip to otherness through objectness.

Dean's *duty* as an explorer in another reality is to broadcast his discoveries as widely as possible. He is producing *communiqués* from The Other Reality. The record cover has shown itself to be the perfect medium for these *communiqués*. As for the originals, they are supremely important to him. They are the journal, the history, the log of his explorations. "I want to realize the world all these drawings are coming from. The drawings have to be there as a first step into that reality."

Donald Lehmkuhl 1974

8

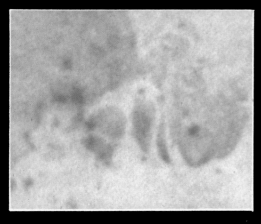  

SOME NOTES ON ROGER DEAN'S TECHNIQUE

Roger Dean has developed a great variety of techniques to enhance his pictures' peculiar quality of a distinct, yet non-photographic, "realism." Among the effects of this is the drawings' property of bearing long and close scrutiny and high magnification (see detail on this page). As is emphasised throughout the explanatory text that accompanies the pictures in this book, a secondary motive behind this was to produce originals which would reproduce well by the method of photolithography. The primary impulse, however, was to render believable what had been considered unbuildable.

A common factor in all of his methods is indicated by Dean's statement that he "would like the technique to be invisible." He takes advantage of the incompatibility of certain media (e.g. wax crayon and inks) to achieve an outline which, like those we impose on our visual sensations, is vibrant and cannot be finally defined. A related technique which exploits the immiscability of water with oil-based paints is a more sophisticated and controlled version of the well-known phenomenon called "marbling." In most cases, this is utilised for its tonal qualities as a background and blends in almost incidentally. Sometimes, however, it may become the subject of the picture.

For instance, in the case of the drawing used for the cover of this book, Dean first "drew" on a white board with water, then sprayed on a succession of oil-based paints (enamel aerosol sprays). By tilting the board this way and that and seeing how the pattern was growing, he was able to produce a surface of great richness and intensity. At this stage the "Green Castle" it was to become had already been visualised and sketched by Dean. Often he would do several boards at once in the same colour scheme and then have them around to stimulate his imagination and to use when the opportunity arose.

In the drawing reproduced on the cover and in detail above, Dean has worked on the "marbled" surface with such sensitivity that it is impossible, in places, to distinguish between the capricious, flowing forms of the paint and his own additions to it. This is analogous to the impossibility of making a final distinction between "nature" and "architecture" in his three-dimensional work.

The eye is led up the path, under the buttresses, through the ascending tunnels, around the structure, behind the visible surface until finally we are, in imagination, exactly where Dean wants us to be — already inside the Castle, where he has been before us.

Dean's habitual method is to work out the design first in a series of sketches. He draws rapidly with a constantly sharpened soft pencil on pads of semi-transparent paper, which allows him to trace and carry through the parts of the design which conform to his original conception, while making modifications to the rest. Sometimes two or three sketches are enough, sometimes it takes dozens to get it right. "Normally I have it right the first time. I do the struggling in hundreds of little sketches. I have the idea right before I draw the first line. The problem then is to reproduce the image which, till then, is flashing complete only in my mind."

This was the method used to draw the dragon and its rider in the "Green Castle" drawing, which were then cut out and stuck on to the board. A faint whitish spray of "dust" around the animals' feet and a suggestion of their shadows in gouache was all that was necessary to complete the atmospheric absorption of the figures into their space.

A great many sketches were made for the Paladin drawing and by looking at a selection of these (pp. 63-64) one may follow the development of the mechanised horse image in some detail. In most cases, the finished drawing bears an astonishing resemblance to the image

conjured up by the first crude sketches, confirming Dean's assertion that the image is "flashing complete" in his mind at the outset. The very first thumbnail sketch for Paladin is reproduced here (approximately actual size) and it is indeed very close to the finished picture in which the horsemen seem to have grown out of the inchoate swirlings of the background. On the same sheet of paper is a memorandum which sums up in words the quality Dean wanted: "Paladin Charge!— cross between spaceman and medieval knight—bolts of electricity from lances—horselike animals but not horses."

In terms of content, Dean's work gains much of its power from the juxtaposition of disparate elements. The same tendency can be seen to be a key factor in his technical procedures. Montage in various forms is indeed the most constant characteristic of his technique, while the relationship between "subject" and "ground" is extremely flexible, and no two pictures have a parallel evolution.

In the case of the "Green Castle" drawing, Dean was consciously trying to direct the flow of the paint into forms suggesting those of his own architecture, later making additions in pencil and water colour which seem to carve out the rock, clarifying the ambiguities and leading us to read the image in the way he has intended. Although the Paladin drawing has a more complex development, and goes through many permutations, it too eventually conforms to the first conception. In the Octopus drawing, (pp.47-48), for the beast itself Dean has grafted the head of a manta ray onto the powerful tentacles. These seem to be stirring up a muddy sea-bed which is in fact an otherwise unmodified piece of "marbling."

Dean is constantly refining and varying the techniques outlined above. Sometimes he reverses the paper and draws the final version in mirror-image on the back of the previous sketch. This is then transferred onto cartridge paper by rubbing. Finally it is delineated in rapidograph, in fine dip pen, or in pencil, in preparation for colouring. (At this stage it may be photographically recorded for black-and-white reproduction.) When doing washes in ink or watercolour, Dean works with a brush in each hand, preventing a line forming as it dries. His use of a combination of different media in the same picture produces unique effects. All these methods are directed towards enhancing the credibility of the images depicted.

Dean draws constantly on a vast collection of visual material: files of cuttings, heaps of magazines and comics, and shelves full of illustrated books. Victorian natural history books rub shoulders with the latest photographic studies in astronomy, geology, plant and animal life. He collects the fine volumes produced during the Edwardian "golden age" of illustrated books in which the binding, the layout and the illustrations are all in accord. All this material can only be regarded as "sources for" or "influences on" Dean's work, in the same sense as can the thousands of colour slides of rock formations, twisted trees etc. he uses as reference material. He also often refers to a collection of old hand-tinted postcards of, for example, waterfalls, pathways and megalithic rocks (e.g. Topographic Oceans pp.116, 117-118). These cards, which combine transparent inks with indistinct photographic images, have a similar atmospheric quality to Dean's own work. Dean denies any direct influences on his work, but says that the North-West coast of Scotland has been a major inspiration.

Although Dean is rarely stuck for an idea, during the actual process of completing a drawing he occasionally loses confidence in its potential effectiveness, especially if the drawing is simple or if it lacks a single focus of attention (e.g. pp.101-102 and 153-154). In these

circumstances, Dean surrounds himself with his own work, the purpose being, he says, to aid confidence. He likes the encouraging phrase from the I Ching: "Perseverance furthers." Dean says that often he has to say to himself "Stay with it, it will speak for itself" when he is tempted to start again with a superficially more arresting foreground. "I often find it reassuring to have examples of my own work around me, so I can see that I have met the problem before."

Roger Dean regrets that he has never studied life drawing and when human figures appear in his work they are usually adapted from photographic sources, including Muybridge. Any available friends may be called in to take up the required pose for an instant Polaroid snap, or to press the trigger while Dean poses himself. Dean finds that he does not often manage to inject sufficient dynamism into his human figures. Occasionally a photograph of a person is physically incorporated into a drawing (pp. 86, 77-78, 153).

The other area that must be mentioned briefly here is that of Dean's lettering and graphic work. Although he is highly articulate, Dean is not primarily a verbal person, and his successes with handwritten texts may be attributed to the fact that he draws the letters rather than writes them, sometimes with reference to some intangible quality he wishes to associate with the words. These started with the handwritten notes for the early

record covers, which happened because he was unfamiliar with the procedures of type-setting. Later he was specifically asked to hand-write the text for such covers as Greenslade and labels such as Fly.

This calligraphic ability found a more condensed expression in Dean's designs for logos (e.g. Osibisa p.53). The title for this book was finally decided upon because it offered the possibility of a very angular lettering form. The pointed VIEWS could be seen as an exclamation mark after his stylised signature. In general, the simpler these verbal motifs are, the better they work, the YES logo being a prime example (pp. 97, 103). Related to these verbal logos or trademarks are the visual symbols which Dean designed within the constraints of a circular format for record labels (e.g. Fly and Virgin, pp. 80, 85, 86, 87). The Harvest label (p. 61) is the earliest of these and it is certainly the purest and most abstract expression of Dean's concern with changes in nature occuring through time.

In trying to write about Roger Dean's work, the constant impulse is to give up and simply present the works to speak for themselves, possessed as they are of a richness and complexity which can only be deminished by the limitations of words. The clarity which characterises his pictures is, by an apparent paradox, ever conveyed by ambiguity.

Dominy Hamilton

Biographical Outline

1944 Roger Dean was born in Ashford, Kent, England, on the 31st of August at 8.30pm. His mother had studied dress design at Canterbury School of Art before her marriage. His father was an engineer in the British army and he took the option of going abroad, so most of Roger Dean's childhood was spent away from England—in Greece, Cyprus and Hong Kong. He has a brother Martyn and two sisters, Penny and Philippa.

1959 The family returned to Britain. Dean went to Ashford Grammar School.

1961 Dean entered Canterbury School of Art to do a three year course in the Industrial Design Department, working towards a National Diploma of Design. He first studied silversmithing, then furniture design.

1964-5 Still at Canterbury, Dean took the one year Intermediate Course. He made the first designs for the "Sea Urchin" chair.

1965 Dean started at the Royal College of Art in London, studying in the Furniture School under Professor David Pye. He made the "Sea Urchin" chair (p. 13) and also designed his house.

1968 Graduated with MDesRCA. Continued to live and work in London. Designed seating for "Upstairs" at Ronnie Scott's Jazz Club. Dean did his first record cover, for a group called Gun (p. 24). He spent the next two years doing odd covers for various record companies while still working on his architectural and furniture projects.

1970 With his brother Martyn, Dean took part in the Daily Telegraph "Design for Living" exhibition at Maples.

1971 In the spring of this year Dean did the first Osibisa cover which attracted a lot of attention. His work began to be sought after by groups and record companies. In November there was a small exhibition, mainly of his architectural drawings, at the Università Internazionale dell'Arte in Florence, where he was invited to give a series of lectures. Late in the same year he did his first cover for YES (p. 97).

1972 Dean and his brother designed a stage set for YES (see p. 125). Early in 1972 Dean moved to Brighton with Dominy Hamilton.

1973 Dean began to work on several film and book projects, including this one.

1975 In August-September he had an exhibition at the New York Cultural Center, which was mostly of his record cover designs. He is currently working on a book of architectural ideas. He is also looking for the ideal site to build his house (see p. 132).

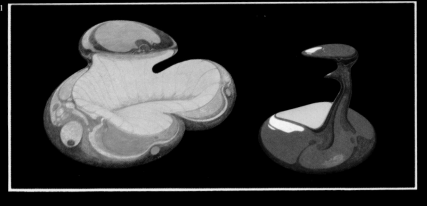

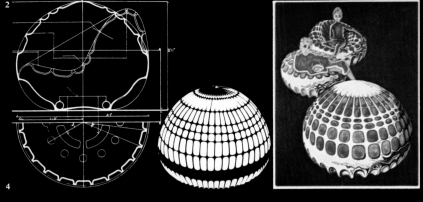

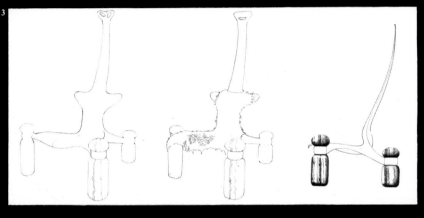

During the seven years he spent at art school (1961-1968) Roger Dean was developing his own ideas within the constraints of an environment committed to the concept of "design," but early on he realised that his interests did not lie within the sphere of design as such. Art schools were intent on preserving the distance between "fine art" and "design"; moreover, "design" itself was subdivided into separate schools. The principles for three-dimensional design were based on a relationship between "function," economics, and technology. The twentieth-century designers' dictum "form follows function" seemed to Dean an empty slogan, if for no other reason than that their definition of function was limited and mechanical. "Technology isn't there for us to design to. We design and then make technology fit. Technology isn't a complete thing, it's merely a tool for the idea." From the first he was very disinterested in the set projects that formed the basis of his early art school training.

These projects were always set and conceived in terms of an existing formal framework. The design process was involved with reworking details on established models. The very idea of designing such a thing as a dining chair seemed pointless to Dean, for although it was occasionally an enjoyable exercise, he felt it was ultimately without consequence as the formal problems

had been resolved five thousand years before.

Dean draws a clear distinction between "design," or the reworking of a pre-existent model, and "invention," the making of something new. The first thoughts about the chair which has come to be known as the "Sea Urchin" were as early as 1965, when Roger Dean was still at Canterbury College of Art. "I started with a vague notion of a chair one could do anything with: one could sit in it in any position, and approach it from any direction." In use the chair is indeed extremely adaptable: if you approach it from a high angle you get a low, reclining position, and if you approach it from a low angle you get an upright position with a firm lumbar support. All results are stable when in position, and very comfortable. Dean says that he still has not "designed" the "Sea Urchin" chair. Apart from the furry cover, which is an interim measure, the "Sea Urchin" is still a basic mechanism.

At Canterbury the chair was not considered a viable proposition by the tutors, who did not think it would work. Dean encountered a similar reaction when, towards the end of his first year at the Royal College of Art, he began to work on it once more. At this time (1966) a competition for designing furniture was sponsored by the British Plastics Federation. Dean decided to enter his chair, and in the spring and summer of that year he made working drawings for it (figs. 4-5). His original design had been in profiled foam (see p. 14), but he was curious about the possibilities of thin-walled plastic structures (nylon or polypropylene). The chair he entered in the competition was a result of these experiments. The chair was unplaced in the competition because it was not believed to be feasible, but it was considered interesting and received some publicity.

During the first term of his second year at the RCA (autumn 1966), pictures of the chair were published in the trade journals. Roger Dean was approached by the

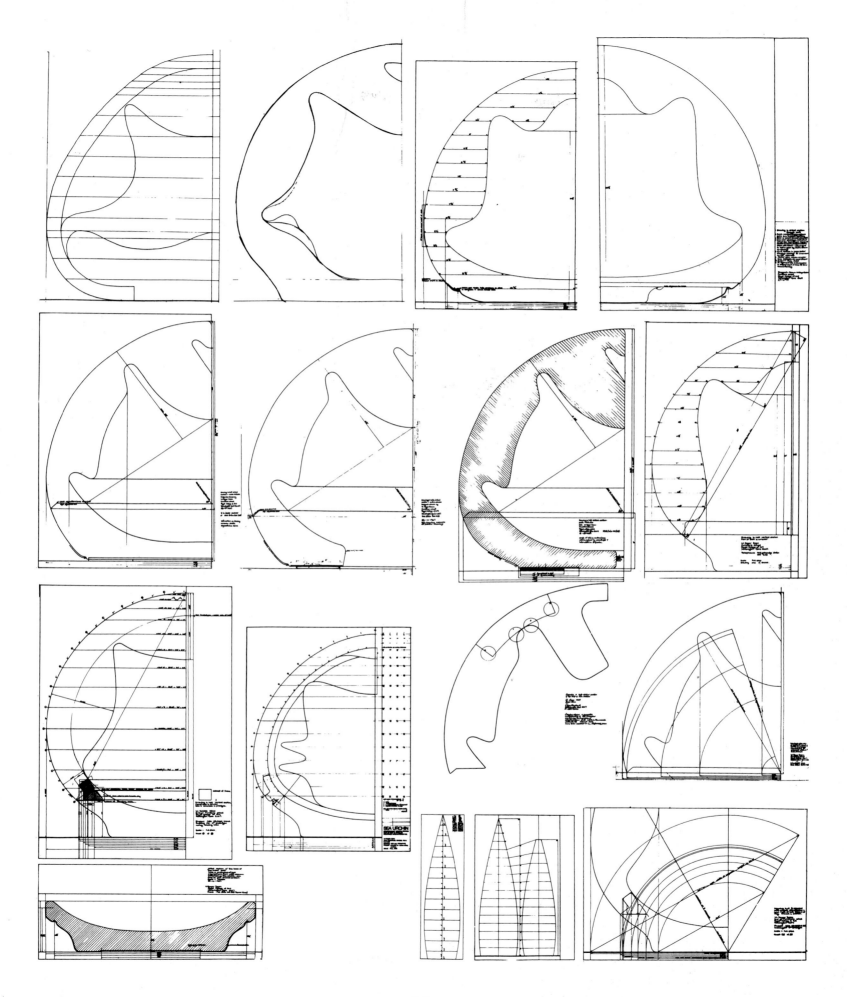

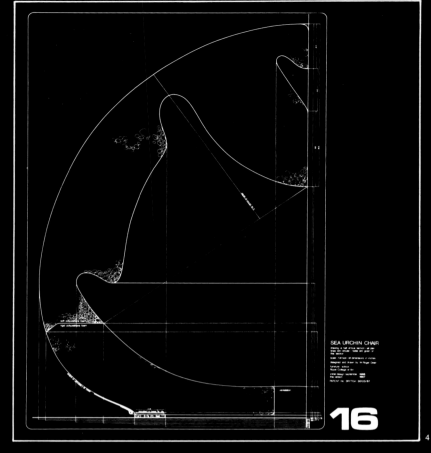

SEA URCHIN CHAIR

16

Design Centre to submit a prototype for an exhibition of "prototype furniture" which was to take place the following January. It was at this point, by chance, that the chair got its name. Someone from the Design Centre referred to it as a "sea anemone" and Dean corrected them: they were thinking of the wrong animal. The chair actually looked like a sea urchin shell without its spines. It is difficult to avoid references to organic forms when discussing Dean's work; he attributes this to the lack of an appropriate vocabulary. This prototype was included in the end of term assessment and, contrary to expectations, it worked very well; the chair moulded itself to the body of the sitter, giving perfect

lumbar support. It was a bit lumpy, "like an old potato," he recalls. He took it home on the train with him and worked on it with a breadknife during the Christmas vacation while his mother made a cover for it. It was included in the Design Centre exhibition and attracted a good deal of acclaim and publicity.

Hille (a furniture manufacturing company) approached Dean and said they would like to manufacture and market it. It was in the adaptation of the handmade prototype into a production model that the inherent difficulties became apparent. There was one great advantage in the idea of moulding the chair: in theory the movement of the foam could be controlled by very precise, idealised profiles. In practice this was out-weighed by one of the disadvantages of working with moulded foam: it flows very badly, which tends to give rise to structural weaknesses. At this time foam technology was still grappling with that problem.

In a continuous density medium like slabstock foam the problem of the hinge area (a quarter of the way down the outside wall shown on sections (p. 14) and the final mould section (p. 15 fig. 4) could be easily resolved because considerations of strength and mobility were complementary with a wall thickness of 2 to 3 inches at

the hinge area. In the moulded foam version, however, the requirements for strength and mobility were un-reconcilable, in that when the wall was thin the foam would not flow properly and tended to bunch up in knots which were structurally very weak. When the wall thickness was increased, not only was mobility impeded, but the tension on the inside surface became critical when sat on. After many attempts (p. 14) a final profile was resolved (p. 15 fig. 4) which seemed to work when combined with improved foam technology. Hille went into limited production with this version (p. 15 figs. 1, 2 and 3). However, while a randomly selected number of production models could stand up to tests simulating the effect of 10 years' use, the failure rate due to bad moulding was too high. Unfortunately it took over 2 years to discover this. During the course of the testing Roger Dean had independently devised a production method that bypassed the problems of moulding in the hinges, but by that time Hille had decided to stop the project.

Closely related to the "Sea Urchin" project was the "Teddy Bear" chair. "The "Teddy Bear" chair was literally just sitting there, demanding its obvious right to exist. I couldn't resist it." Roger Dean designed and built

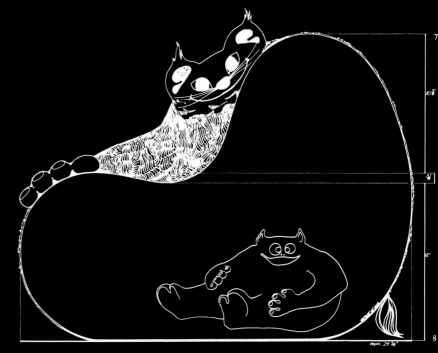

the first prototype himself (p.16 figs. 6, 7). Hille were shown the design and although they liked the idea, they felt it was not appropriate for their market as contract furnishers. At this time Roger and his brother Martyn were asked to submit designs for an exhibition sponsored by The Daily Telegraph Magazine and

Maples, called "Experiments in Living." Roger Dean decided to use the exhibition as a show-place for the chair and several other projects he and his brother were already working on. He then met a manufacturer who was interested in producing the chair. Since there was not enough time for a fully-fledged prototype programme, they decided to cast the chair for the exhibition in solid chip-foam. Dean knew that this would be impracticable for mass-production because they would use too much material, and so be too heavy for children to move without pulling their ears and arms off. In anticipation of this problem, Dean designed a much lighter chair (a 2 inch skin of foam on a vacuum-formed shell). Unfortunately this was never built because the chair was such a success that the manufacturer decided to go straight into production with the chair in its solid form. The manufacturer abandoned the project shortly after because it seemed the chairs would be too expensive and too heavy. Roger Dean still harbours a dream that one day the "Teddy Bear" chairs will live again.

The "Teddy Bear" chair did not utilize any of the structural principles of the "Sea Urchin." The first project to explore the flexibility of the "Sea Urchin's" versatile mechanism came out of the requirements of a living-room seating for a house scheme. (This scheme is discussed in some detail later in the book). The requirements for this living-room were that the seating should have a focal point (a fire-place, for instance), while maintaining a certain complexity of structure which would enable a number of different activities to be carried out in it simultaneously. It had to be complete in itself, and not feel empty when it was not full. The intricate structure provided areas of privacy as well as more dynamic spaces.

Dean felt that his first sketches of the seating were not clear enough (p. 18 fig. 3). "I was still grappling with the problem of how to draw. Up to now the drawing techniques that were suitable for conventional designs being done both in art schools and professionally, whether they were for architecture or silversmithing, were very linear. It was an established

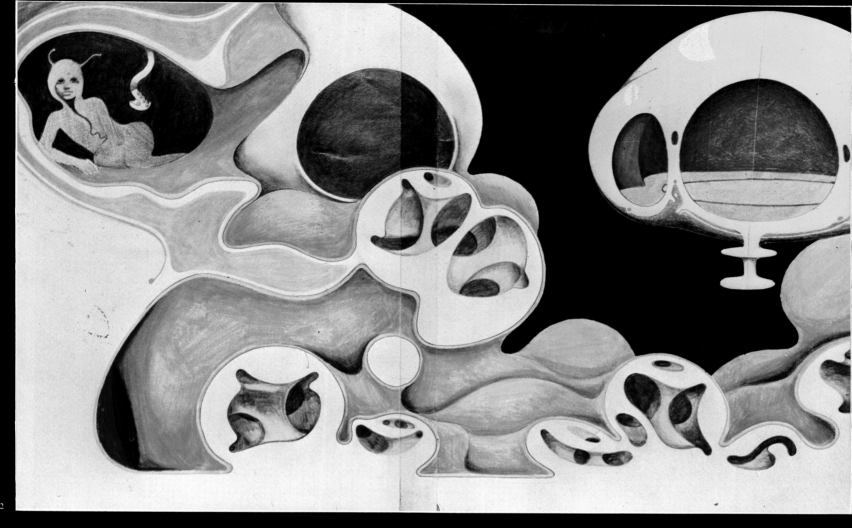

2

3

language: we understood the shapes implied by the outlines. The "Sea Urchin" chair did not present a problem either as a perspective drawing or as a technical drawing. Whether the drawings were good or bad, they could be understood. The fact that people did not think the chair would work was not because the drawings did not contain the relevant information, but because of their lack of understanding of the structural principles involved."

"When I first drew the green landscape seating pictures (pp. 17, 18 figs. 1, 2) the problem was how to describe the forms in a sketch. My concern was not to make a pretty picture, but merely to convey the information. I had almost no formal training in drawing, and had to develop these techniques. The second problem that arose out of this was that the convention of technical drawing would have become severely overloaded by having to portray the very complex curvilinear forms. Whereas curved shapes can be described, like cars or boats, they are often much simpler and we have learned to anticipate their geometry."

"Interestingly enough, my brother, who was at the Central School of Art, was faced with the same problems at just about the same time, but it was not until much later that we ever got together to talk about them. Martyn's approach was slightly different from mine. He basically decided to bypass the drawing stage and to go straight into the three-dimensional model and prototype, although of course he did some

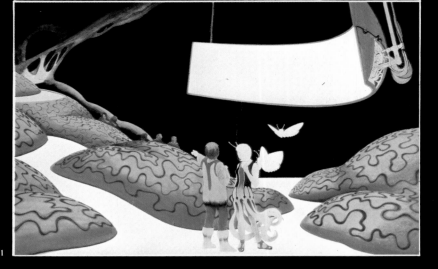

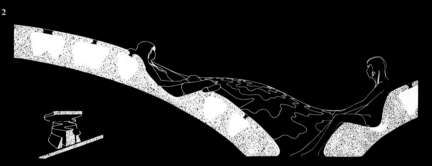

drawings. I tried to resolve the problem firstly in two dimensions. One of the consequences of this was that Martyn had a much more sophisticated grasp of the problems involved in getting his projects realised. Over the next few years, as we began to work on projects together, he continually got at me about something which I was unaware of at the time: that it simply wasn't enough to be creative on paper. The conception was only a part of the creative act; one then had to follow the project through to its final state, whatever we decided that should be. Each project had to be taken to the stage where it generated its own momentum. What we had to learn were the techniques involved in getting it to that stage, and how to recognize it when we got there. Often it wasn't enough to build a prototype or even have a limited production run."

The green landscape seating and many other early drawings came from a sketchbook that Dean started using at the RCA, just after he left Canterbury. In this sketchbook Dean recorded and stored for later use, ideas which he had begun to work on but did not have the time to develop fully. Of the drawings and ideas to be stored in the book, some were for three-dimensional projects that he intended to build at a later stage, while others were closer to fantasy. The most recent of these

to be developed was used for the "Relayer" album (see p. 122 fig. 1 and pp. 123, 124).

In the drawings of the green landscape seating the possibilities for developing the "Sea Urchin's" structure became apparent. "They had the wrong feel for a living-room and, more crucially, the wrong scale. But instead of abandoning these drawings as failures, I found them leading me towards the larger-scale concepts of landscape seating. In fact this was the first time I had thought of seating in terms of 'landscape.'"

Dean's first experiments in landscape seating were for auditoriums. Once again he entered a competition. It was for foam furniture, sponsored by Dunloprene. The structural principles of the "Sea Urchin" chair were far too complex for this competition, so he devised a new system which was much simpler to make and understand (p. 19 figs. 1, 2). Dean's idea for the auditorium was to provide sloping hill shapes which would collapse when sat on, giving good lumbar and seat support. Dean's idea went unplaced on the grounds that it would not be feasible although, as had happened before with other projects, it aroused a good deal of interest. Prototypes of sections of seating were in fact built by Dean himself a year later, and they worked very well. Dean worked on ideas for a number of different seating terrains. One of these, which was never built, was designed to be walked through rather like low shrubs whose flexible "foliage" could be turned into stable seats when pushed in a certain way. This would have been quite different from his competition entry, which had very specific aisles and pathways.

Soon after working on the plans for the auditorium he redrew the living-room of the house (p. 19 fig. 3), controlling the scale and fitting the furniture into a

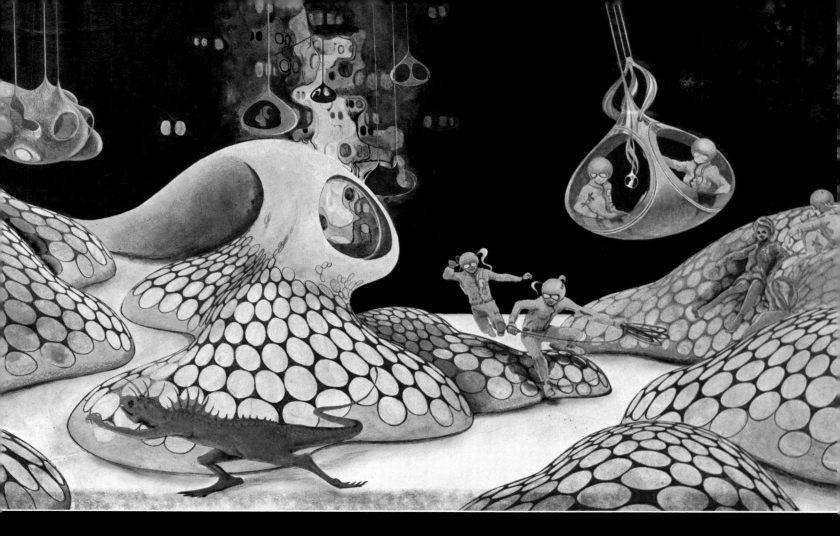

drawing of the room taken from the model of the house (p. 135). Dean does not feel that he has been able to fully explore the possibilities of landscape seating. He has plans to develop some of the variations in the future, and he is continually thinking about it. His latest drawing for continuous foam seating is on the Steve Howe album cover (p. 153-154).

The blue landscape (p. 20) is a view of the interior of one of Roger Dean's architectural projects. "The 'city' was like a huge hill with houses built on the outside, and with a giant 'cave' on the inside. The floor of the 'cave' had its own landscape, part of which was this seating. The object containing two figures which is seen hanging from the roof of the structure is a lift. It is controlled by the occupants and moves horizontally as well as vertically. The light in the background is daylight, and one of the lift-pods is seen in silhouette against it. It is on its way out of the 'cave.'" (An external view of this structure is shown on page 145, figure 1).

During his Diploma show at the Royal College of Art

Dean met the director of a furniture company which coincidentally, was taken over by the Hille group the following year. He was interested in the landscape seating and asked Dean if he would be prepared to do some work for his company. They wanted him to design the seating for Ronnie Scott's new "Upstairs." The job was done in conjunction with Sean Murphy and Ian Knight, who did the lighting. Sean Murphy later became manager of Soft Machine, and Ian Knight now does Led Zeppelin's stage lighting. Bob Ludman, a technical adviser at Dunloprene who had previously worked with Dean on the foam technology of the "Sea Urchin," also collaborated on this project.

At first Roger Dean was very excited about the project but later he became somewhat frustrated by the constraints of the brief and budget. One of the difficulties he faced was that he had to seat a large number of people in a very small room, while leaving enough space for dancing. Another problem was that they wanted his design to be even simpler than the

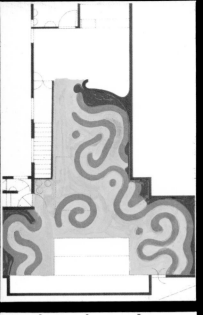
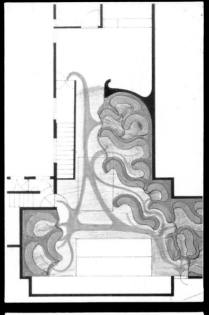

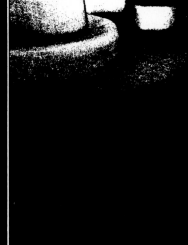

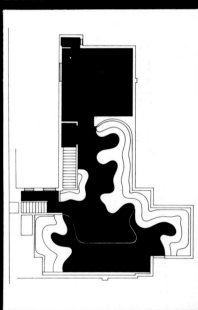

auditorium seating he had entered in the competition. In fact, they were concerned about the design being any more complicated than layers of terraced foam. What is more, it had to be built on an extremely low budget, and in only two weeks. However, this was Dean's first opportunity to actually make a form of landscape seating and see it in use (on this page).

Dean himself worked on the construction.

The work was still being finished as the audience began to arrive on opening night. "At first people stood around and just wondered. It took a while for their inhibitions to break down, and allow them to clamber all over it. Once they started they obviously really enjoyed it. By the end of the evening, when people had overcome their initial reaction of surprise, they started to settle into it, and it worked as I had hoped it would: there were peaceful areas as well as active areas. They understood."

During the building of the seating for the club, Roger Dean showed Jimmy Parsons, a director of Ronnie Scott Directions Ltd., the sketchbook he had worked on at the RCA. He wanted to show him the kind of landscape that could have been done had there been less restrictions. While they were leafing through the book Parsons saw the drawing reproduced on page 22. This drawing was first done to give a visual symbol of what might be imagined as a primeval contrast to the domestic security of the house project (explored at length in his Master's thesis). Parsons was just beginning to manage a band called Gun, and he asked if the drawing could be used for the cover of their first album, since they had just made a record which became a big hit called "Race with the Devil."

Dean decided to start another drawing for the cover and this took him two months to complete. Up until this stage most of his drawings were in pencil, crayon, and pen-and-ink. Because this was to be a picture in its own right, he lavished a variety of media on the Gun

drawing: pencil, wax crayons, gouache, and finally many layers of coloured inks. This gave it a very richly glazed picture surface, which in the original is quite startling. It also gave him his first lesson in what not to do, because it never reproduced satisfactorily. All reproduction techniques captured either the surface or the base colours, but seemed unable to get both. Even for this book this colour plate (p. 23) gave the most trouble. After doing the Gun cover, Roger Dean did some simple line graphics for "Upstairs:" the head and the beckoning figure for the membership card.

Dean has never felt completely at ease working in two dimensions, and he found it difficult to adjust to the new experience of making two-dimensional pictures that had to stand up in their own right, rather than as preliminary drawings for three-dimensional projects. For the first time he also had to tackle the problems of laying out text and typography. He had never even heard of ems or point sizes, and the new discipline exhausted him. Dean has never fully resolved his difficulties about working exclusively in two dimensions, although he has mastered the art of typography. After the early covers, which were experiments in graphic design, the three-dimensional projects began to reappear as subject matter in a pictorial context.

When drawing pictures for his three-dimensional projects he rarely resisted including a monster or two, and yet in this picture of monsters in hell, he couldn't resist a clown or two. (p. 24). After completing the album cover for Gun, Roger Dean still had a few dragons that had to be got out of his system before going on to other things. The hairy monster was an early drawing from the sketchbook. The monsters in a cave were done in the wake of the Gun cover. Dean never expected this picture to be used because it was drawn across a double page of his sketchbook and there are folds down the middle. At this point Dean thought he might like to do some more drawings for record covers, and he began to draw some pictures for a portfolio. The dragon on page 25 is one of these which has never been reproduced before.

The first few record covers Dean did after Gun were for Ronnie Scott Directions. They were on the Vertigo label and were for bands like Nucleus and Keith Tippett, who were very much jazz-orientated. The art director on these records, Mike Stamford, then asked Dean to do some other albums and with the exception of the Keith Tippett album these all used graphic designs rather than illustrations (pp. 29, 30).

Although Roger Dean was having some success with these covers he was beginning to feel that he had been type-cast as a jazz cover designer. Mike Stamford was more interested in the graphic design than in the illustrated covers, and he felt that Dean was better at the graphics. Dean took a break from record covers to work with his brother on the Maples/Telegraph exhibition. Several months later when he started doing covers again he made a decision that pictorial covers were the kind that he was most interested in doing.

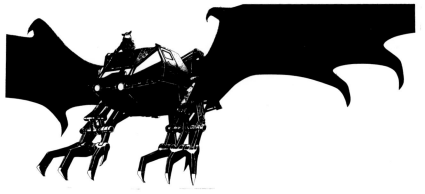

minimal dot of the lithographic printing process did not fade out into white but formed a line (scarring). Dean still had a lot to learn about drawing specifically for reproduction purposes. He was more satisfied with the effect of the line drawing which he enjoyed doing and only took him one hour. The same plane was the subject of many experiments in technique and background. The plane in the large picture is mounted on a background which was his first experiment in the use of enamel spray. He had no airbrush at this time and used aerosol cans. The small picture is superimposed on a photograph. Neither of these was ever reproduced, but the silhouette was used for the inside of the Clear Blue Sky cover. Both of these were derived from the plane which was later to become Dean's trademark and which is shown at the beginning of this book.

The picture of battling flying machines was an early illustrated cover done for a band called Clear Blue Sky. Once again the technique did not reproduce very well although it is much simpler than the Gun drawing, using only pencil and watercolour. This was because the

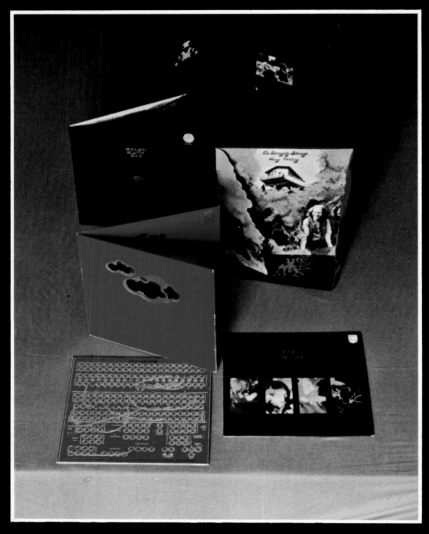

The pictures above are some early covers with a bias towards graphic design: 1 Inside of second Nucleus cover; 2 First Nucleus cover; 3 John Dummer's "Blue"; 4 and 7 Dr. Strangely Strange's "Heavy Petting"; 5 Junco Partners; 6 Graham Collier's "Mosaics."

Figure 9 is the front cover for Ramases' album "Space Hymns." It shows what is apparently a rocket ship, and it is only when the album is opened out that it can be seen to be a church steeple (fig. 8). The idea was Ramases' and they supplied Dean with a very complete rough to work from.

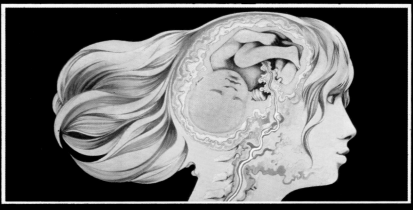

Figure 10 was the cover for a re-released album by Gracious! When their album was first released it featured an exclamation mark, so Dean worked this image into a drawing.

Figure 11 is a line drawing done with a Rapidograph and copied from a photograph. It was used on the back of the second Nucleus album. Roger Dean never found it easy to achieve a good likeness, and he does not really like drawing portraits.

Figure 12 is the cover for the Keith Tippett album "Dedicated to you, but you weren't listening." It was designed jointly by Roger and Martyn Dean. The line drawings below (fig. 14) were from the inside of the album. With the exception of "Space Hymns," which was drawn 50% smaller than its reproduction size, all the drawings shown here were drawn the same size as the album covers.

This tree was done in 1970 for a Dutch band called Earth and Fire. Dean originally intended to use the picture on page 35 for the album, but there was a change in plans at the eleventh hour and the tree was done in one night: Dean began it at 9 in the evening, and finished it by 9 the next morning. It was drawn and used on the cover the other way up but Dean has always preferred it the way it is shown here. The design for the cover was deceptively complex, for there was a figure of a girl walking along a burning shore (p. 31 fig. 2) which was hidden behind the tree roots on the inside of the double layer of board. It could only be seen if the cover was dismantled. Dean is not sure how many people ever found it. The idea of hiding drawings away in a cover has always appealed to Dean. "One day I would like to design a cover which appeared to be completely blank but which actually had the drawings glued into the space between the boards."

Roger Dean did three related drawings for the first cover for a band called Lighthouse. Of these only the first two are shown here (pp. 33-34); the third mysteriously disappeared between the printer and the record company, a fate that was to befall several other pictures. Lighthouse is a Canadian band and Mike Stamford wanted to re-package the album for the European market. Dean was asked to re-design the cover. The two drawings on page 32 were each done about 13 inches square (i.e. approximately the size they were intended to be reproduced), and they were used for the second cover which was also a re-packaging brief. This continues the theme of the first: the sea retreats and land appears with the passage of time. The idea of successive pictures telling a story appealed to him and he was to use it several times. "Often when I was drawing I worked out a complex story structure to fit around the picture. I found it helped me maintain consistency."

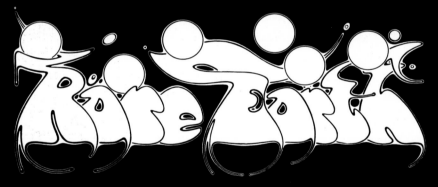

The picture on page 35 was used on a cover for Rare Earth, a white band on the Motown label and one of their biggest acts. Dean was recommended by John Marshall at Motown to go and see Ron Strasner, the group's manager, when he was in England. He was very anxious to use this drawing, which Dean had in fact started for Earth and Fire, but there was a great rush to finish it because the album was already cut. Dean was given about a week to finish and deliver the art-work to them in Detroit. Unfortunately it did not arrive in time and had to appear as an inside spread. It is one of the very few of Dean's pictures that are consciously derived from a specific source: in this case a collection of Chinese postage stamps which he had picked up when he was in Hong Kong as a boy (1957-59).

In February, 1973, after he had done this cover, Dean went to Los Angeles to meet the band and to discuss future projects. He was completely amazed by L.A. but his one disappointment was Disneyland. He found America very stimulating and did a lot of work as a consequence of the trip. The picture used as the cover of this book and the blue demon on page 83 date from this time. The Rare Earth logo was done on his return to England and was only ever used there.

"What I was trying to do in these pictures was to make a spaceship out of an amalgamation of an insect and a machine. I wanted them to be ambiguous. Were they animals or machines? This is something I have tried to do many times in many different ways (p. 59 fig. 3 and p.67)."

"If a design 'works,'" says Roger Dean, "it should look irreducible. It should be essentially itself: an archetypal form. Very few objects achieve this quality of objectness; we know them when they do. In nature, objectness is not visible in everything. We bring the same faculties to bear in our recognition of objectness in natural forms as we do in man-made ones. In western culture, however, the criteria are not the same. In the ancient art of Feng-Shui the Chinese magicians used to recognise not only that it was possible for nature to get it wrong, but that when the error was diagnosed it was essential to correct it even on the scale of whole land-scapes and mountain ranges."

In many of his designs Dean is concerned with what is essentially a light-hearted game. The only rule of this game is that the elements, however ambiguous they

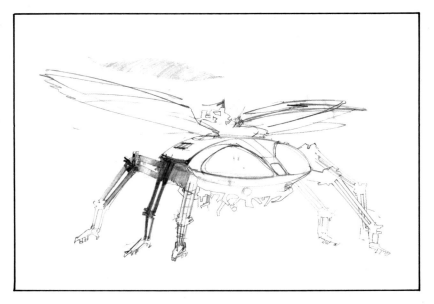

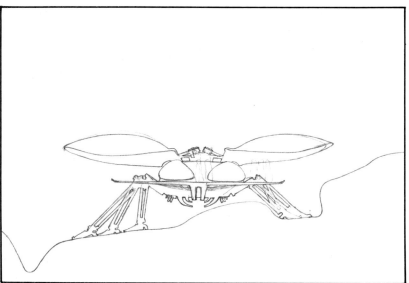

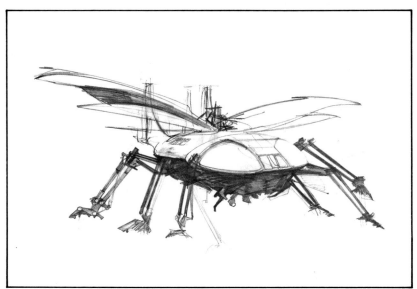

may be, should exist without question. They have their own conviction and when they are made one never feels the need for alteration or improvement. Roger Dean finds no anomaly in applying this philosophy to his serious projects (such as plans for "landscaped" urban areas) or to a piece of furniture.

Like the drawings on the previous page, the two "spaceships" shown here were not done for any particular client. They were used at a later date for Motown's "Chartbusters Volume 6." The blue image was the front cover and the small red one was the back. This picture is probably unique in Dean's oeuvre for being the only time that he has ever re-drawn a picture after it has been used because he was not satisfied with it. On this occasion he re-drew the idea about a month after the cover was finished, and the result was the picture on page 39. It was published by Big "O" with the blue cover drawing as one of a pair of posters.

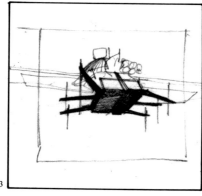

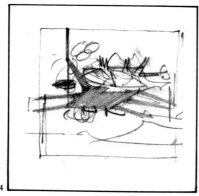

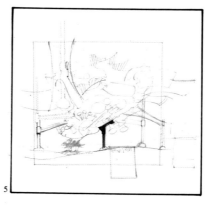

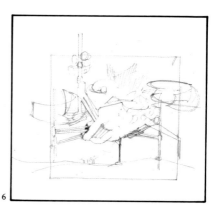

None of the drawings on pages 41-46 were commissioned; they were records of ideas. The walking machines (p. 41 figs. 1, 2) are from the RCA sketchbook. They were done simply for the fun of drawing machines. The purple one started to be developed into a giant walking-music-machine-cum-travelling-stage (figs. 3-7). This was envisaged as being many times larger than the machine in the original drawing, but it was never taken beyond the provisional sketch stage. However, in collaboration with his brother Martyn, Roger Dean did work on a large travelling stage that was designed to be carried on three basic lorries, with

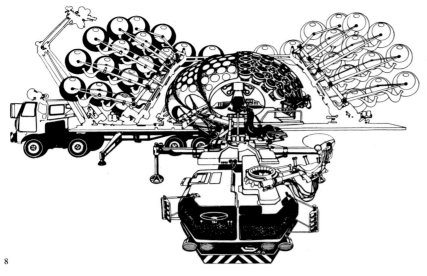

8

two subsidiary lorries carrying the static instruments: (not shown here) the keyboards/organs, and drums. These would have included giant mechanical acoustic instruments as well as electrical instruments. The three basic lorries contained a folding 50 foot stage plus lighting, amplification, and speakers. The spherical speakers shown at the sides of the drawings (pp. 42, 43, 44) were mobile, and were designed to be orientated either towards an audience that was in front of the stage or towards an audience in the round. They could also move during the concert to give a phasing effect. It could all be driven straight into a field or stadium and set up automatically by one person at a central control. It was proposed that all mechanisms should be remote-controlled hydraulics. Besides the obvious convenience for travelling and setting up, the main reason for designing the stage was to provide a dynamic visual focus for large outdoor concerts where often the performers can barely be seen. This problem of scale, incidentally, was a major factor which the Deans had to take into consideration when they were designing the stages for YES. The sketches show a proposal for stage lighting (fig. 9); a fibreglass lighting truss (fig. 10); a canopy (fig. 11); and organ pipes (fig. 12). Some of the ideas from this period were later taken up and developed for the YES stages.

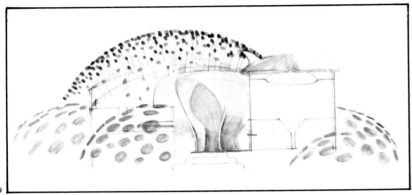

9

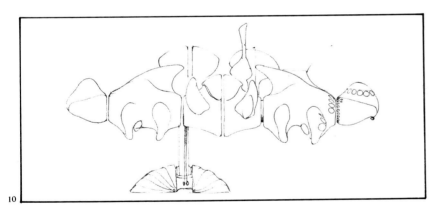

10

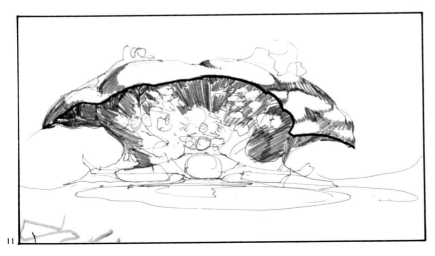

11

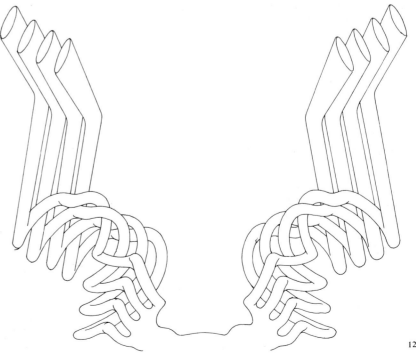

12

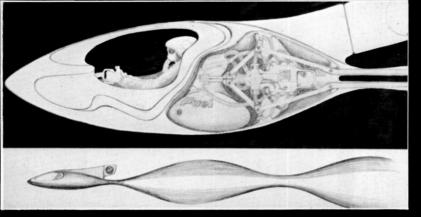

The submarines (fig. 1) were designed as part of a project for a floating city which Dean abandoned. Dean thinks they probably would not work as well as submarines with conventional propellers, but he liked the idea of them swimming. Dean's submarines had two tails which moved in opposition, powered by hydraulic rams which moved the central spines of these tails.

Among the myriad wheeled vehicles which Dean has designed are the amphibious jeep, and the mini-jeep, which is based on the chasis of a Hillman "Imp." These were inspired by Dean's enormous collection of Dunlop rubber car-tyre ashtrays (6 inches in diameter), which had been given to him during his foam projects. He had always wanted to make models which would utilize these ashtrays, and these were detailed drawings of projected plans which never actually got made.

Dean enjoys the idea of exploiting the dynamic qualities of machines and emphasising them for expressive purposes. He particularly likes steam loco-motives and the earth movers that must have struck many of us in our more imaginative moods as being inescapably dinosaur-like. These drawings were

slightly tongue-in-cheek design projects and they are included here to make the point that there is no absolute demarcation line between Dean's viable projects and the designs that people tend to think of as pure "fantasy."

These drawings are for a project which Dean took much more seriously, and to which he devoted a good deal of time and energy during his time at the RCA. The red tractor (fig. 5) carried with it the means of making a giant sphere around itself approximately ten

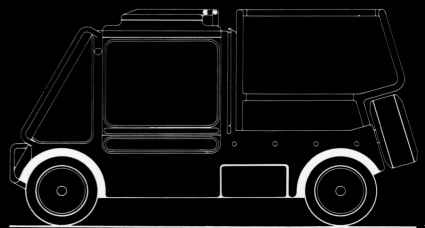

The picture on the following pages was for Gentle Giant's album "Octopus."

5

times its own length (fig. 6). Two models were made, one of which had a pneumatic sphere, the other a rigid geodesic sphere. The first tractor model was about 6 inches long, with a 4 foot diameter transparent inflatable sphere. It manoeuvred quite satisfactorily across a "landscape" of upturned chair legs. Its moving principle is rather like a universal "bridge." The driver of the tractor can ignore the bridge's existence and steer wherever he wants to go; the bridge will be there. It could be used to cross forests, swamps, or even slow-moving traffic.

The caterpillar mechanism (fig. 7) was designed to work in conjunction with a snow-sledge, allowing it to drive up a snow-covered hill and slide down the other side. The principle upon which it worked was a rotating track (moving clockwise in this drawing) within a flexible non-rotating "sleeve." The "sleeve" (white area) narrowed at the underside to the width of the rollers that were spaced alternately on long and short flanges. When in action this produced a wave motion on the shovel feet, creating a crawling effect across the snow.

6

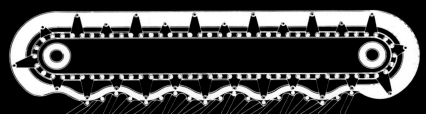

7

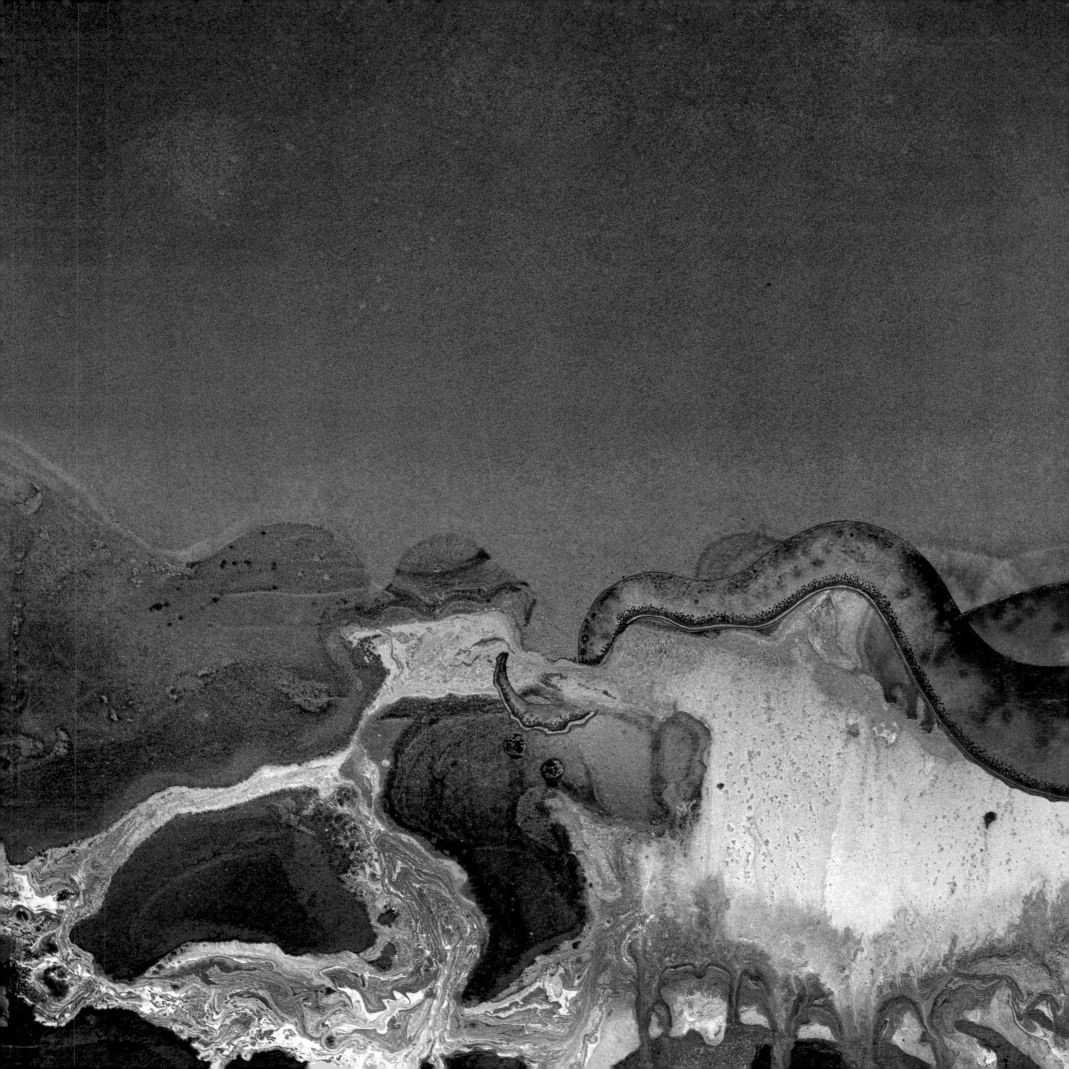

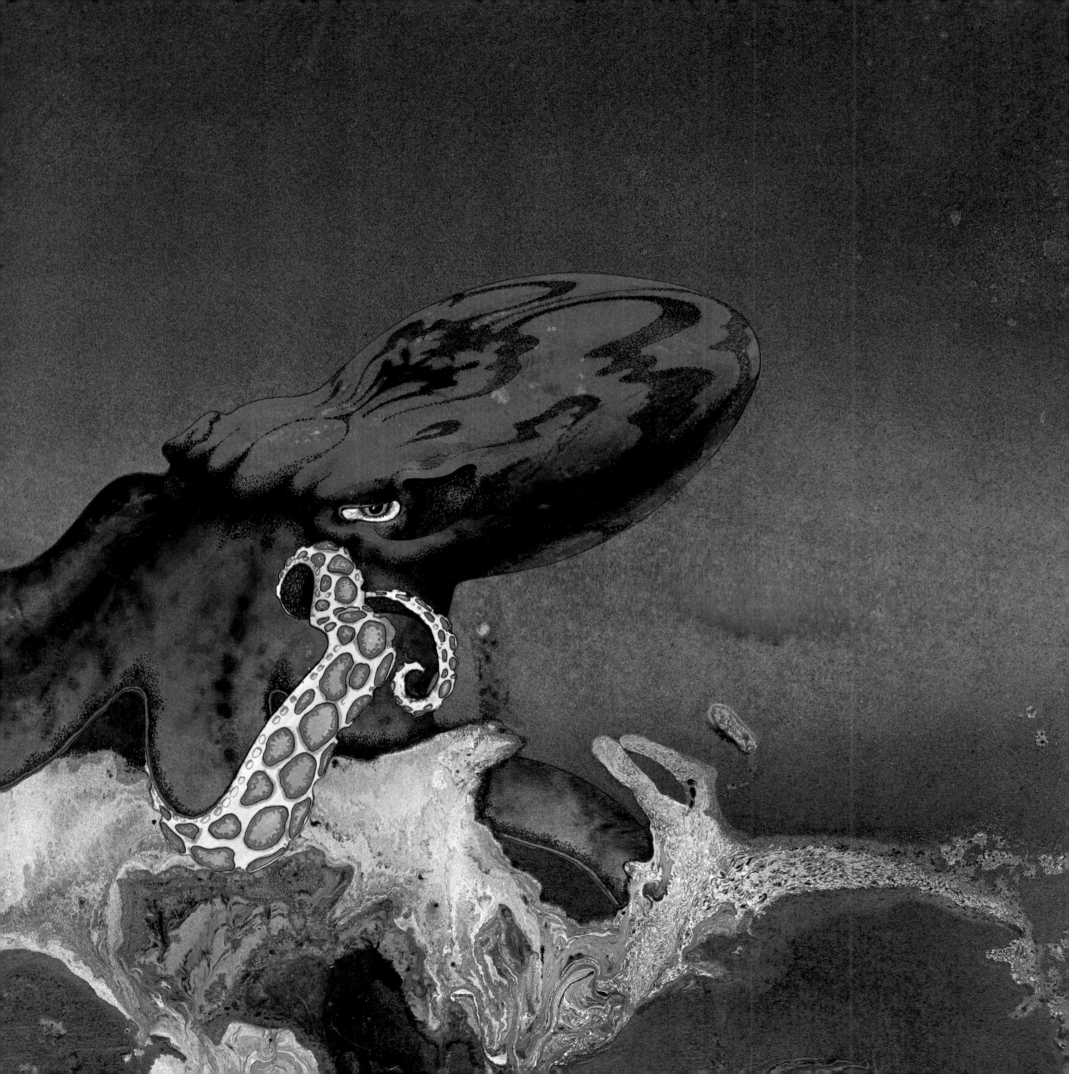

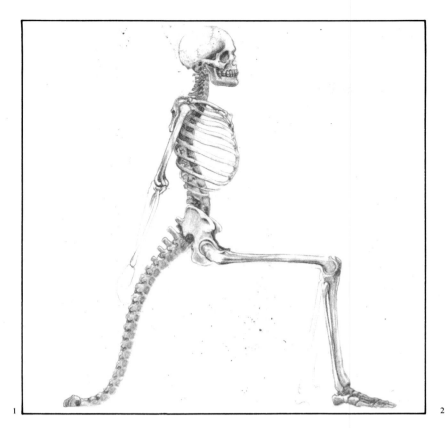

The first album cover for Midnight Sun (p. 50 fig. 2), a Scandinavian band, was designed for them while they still intended to call themselves the Rainbow Band, but another group used the name first. Dean also did a poster for this album (fig. 3). Their second album was called "Walking Circles" (p. 49). The cover design was based on a drawing from the RCA sketchbook (fig. 1). Dean decided that after 5,000 years of chair design the only sufficiently different variation as yet unattempted, as far as he knew, was the bio-chemical approach. Dean's proposal was based on a mechanism favoured by lizards for re-growing their tails. Dean finally abandoned this project because of lack of facilities.

The first Osibisa cover was done for David Howells, whom Roger Dean had met at CBS when he was doing the Gun cover. Howells was now A&R man for MCA in England. The picture shown here (pp. 51, 52) is the final form as it appeared on the cover. Two earlier versions were made which David Howells was not happy with. Because Dean thought the first one was right (and he still maintains that it was), he couldn't start again with it still in existence, so he felt he had to destroy it. However, he did save all the original elephants and incorporated them into the final drawing, although some are hidden by reeds which are superimposed on top.

This cover was undoubtedly the one that did most to establish Dean's reputation; it was enormously successful and the flying elephant motif found its way

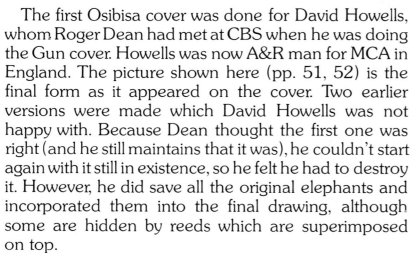

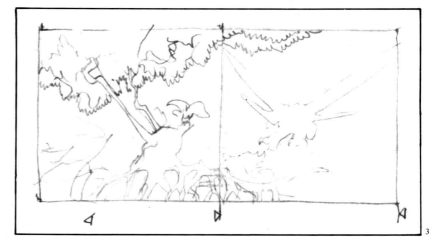

onto T-shirts, badges, an Amsterdam café front, and a hot-air balloon in Denver, Colorado, made by Don Miller. This was also the first time Dean's typography was successful in its own right. It has been widely copied. The Japanese logo, not done by Dean, works very well because it looks so much like the Osibisa logo.

The second cover for Osibisa met with a similar problem. This time the first version (p. 53 fig. 2 and p. 54) was used, but not until it had been initially rejected and a second one had been done (p. 53 fig. 1). It was not until after some debate that it was agreed that the same image would work carried through onto the second album. The second drawing is reproduced re-drawn on pages 145-6. The sketches (page 53) are shown here slightly enlarged. They were the original thumbnail sketches.

Dean played around with the elephant theme and made many drawings and models, but he did not do any more covers for Osibisa. One of the many projects he experimented with was the elephant with a tank head. He envisaged an army of these at war with the

flying elephants. (A plan for a film of this never materialised). When Del Richardson, guitarist from Osibisa, left to make a solo album, he and David Howells asked Dean to do the cover (p. 56). This was done in a very different style from the Osibisa cover although it had a similar feel to it.

Budgie had already had one album released on MCA
when Dean was asked to do their second album. It was
hoped that they could use a photograph of a model he
had made some years before (p. 59 fig. 3). The model
was based on a plastic kit with the top part of a
seagull's skull moulded into the front. The basic idea
for the model is the same as the elephant with the
tank head; on seeing the end-products the relationship
between animal and machine is obvious.

Dean made many attempts to photograph the model
plane. The sort of perspective he wanted is shown on
page 59 (figs. 4, 5). Unfortunately, even stopped right

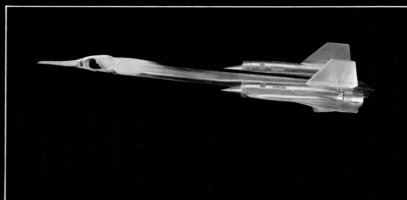

down to f.64 on a plate-camera, there was insufficient
depth of field to get the whole 18 inch model in focus.
The only photographs that worked were those showing
a side elevation (p. 58) so, ironically, he ended up
doing a drawing of it.

The drawings for Budgie's third album are also shown
here (p. 59 figs. 1, 2). The coloured one which was
used for the cover is 24 inches by 12 inches, and
incorporates the Budgie figure from their first album,
which was not designed by Dean.

These drawings were for Magna Carta's album
'The Lord of Ages.'

Dean designed the Harvest logo soon after he did the Gun cover. He was asked to do it via "Hipgnosis," who designed, for example, all Pink Floyd covers on that label. But it was several years before he actually got around to doing the covers on this page for them.

The Macbeth cover was for the soundtrack of Polanski's movie, and is based on the three witches' scene at the beginning of the play. Dean felt they had got the imagery wrong on this and on many other of

in interpreting the picture.

Babe Ruth's "First Base" was the only other cover done on the Harvest label. He introduced Alan Shacklock to Nick Mobbs from Harvest, and was subsequently asked to do this cover. It was the band's idea to have the baseball theme.

The cover for Paladin "Charge!" was done for Bronze records who were also the management company for Osibisa. Dean made many sketches before he felt he had found the image he was searching for. Those shown here (p. 63-64) are but a few. "I knew the final effect that I wanted and this remained constant throughout. It was the details that took so much time. This happens frequently; I have an initial image that

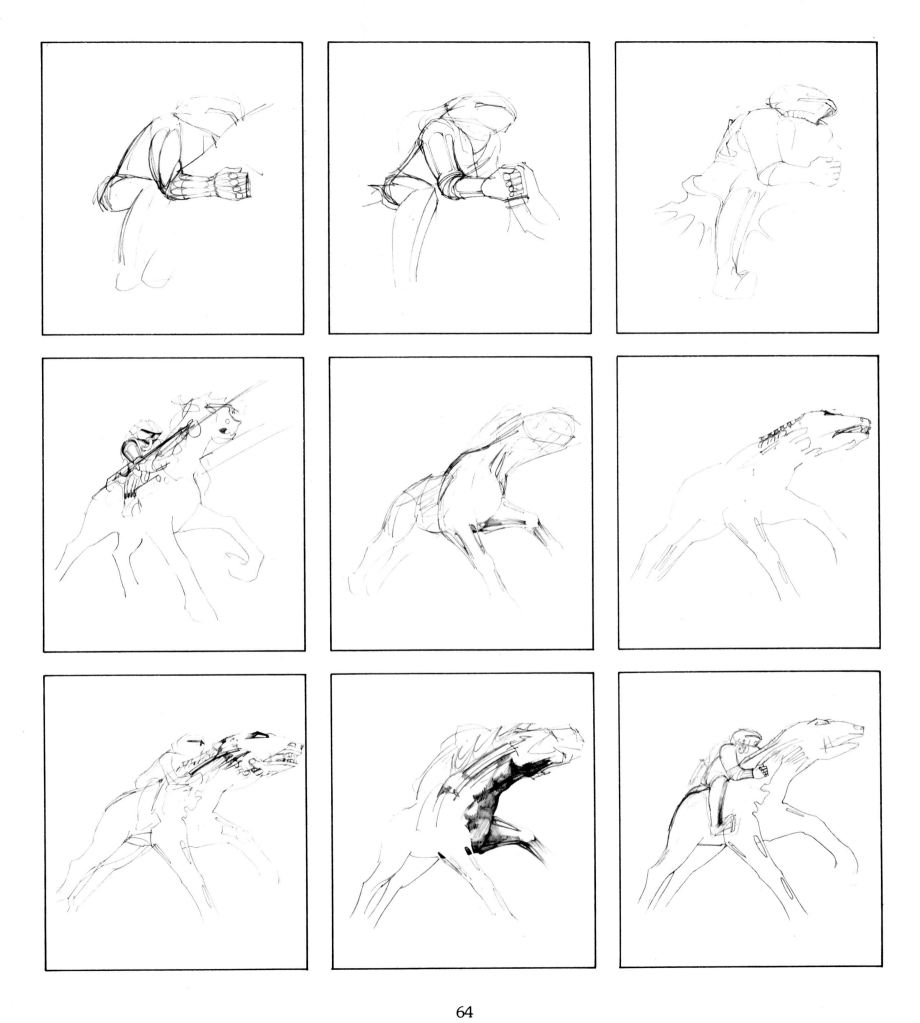

The picture on page 67 was a cover for Nitro Function, and the small bat-wing plane (fig. 1, p. 68) was the back of the same album. The Paladin and Nitro Function drawings were extensions of the same theme, and Dean says that he hopes to develop this imagery further sometime in the future. The cover of Uriah Heep's "The Magician's Birthday" (pp. 71-72) was assembled from the three separate images shown on this page (figs. 3, 4, 5,. Because it had to be completed in a day Dean had to specify the background colour tones he wanted to the printers over the telephone. There was no time to check proofs, and he was relieved to see that the different elements had fused more or less as he had hoped they would. Part of the drawing on pages 69-70 was used for the cover of Uriah Heep's "Demons and Wizards," and a much larger segment of

it is reproduced here. The picture is an allegory of cosmic eroticism: the source of the waterfall signifying that of all life in time. Before Dean had finished the cover he broke his right wrist, and the rainbow demon (fig. 2) had to be painted with his left hand.

URIAH HEEP
THE MAGICIAN'S
BIRTHDAY

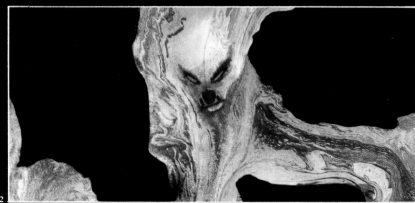

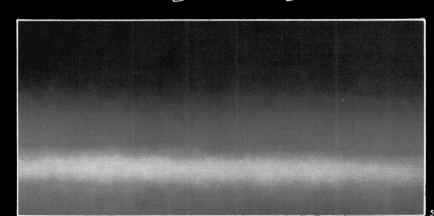

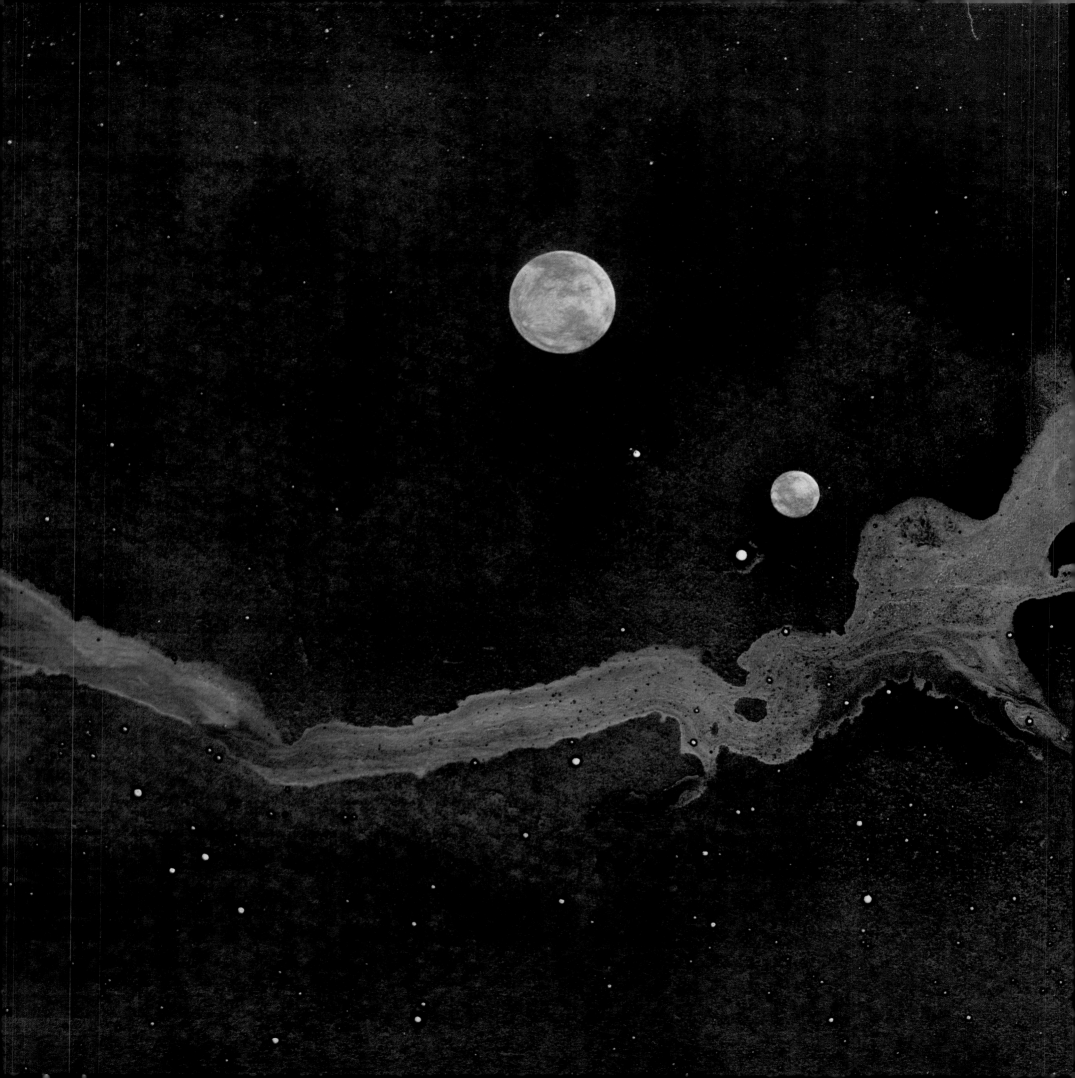

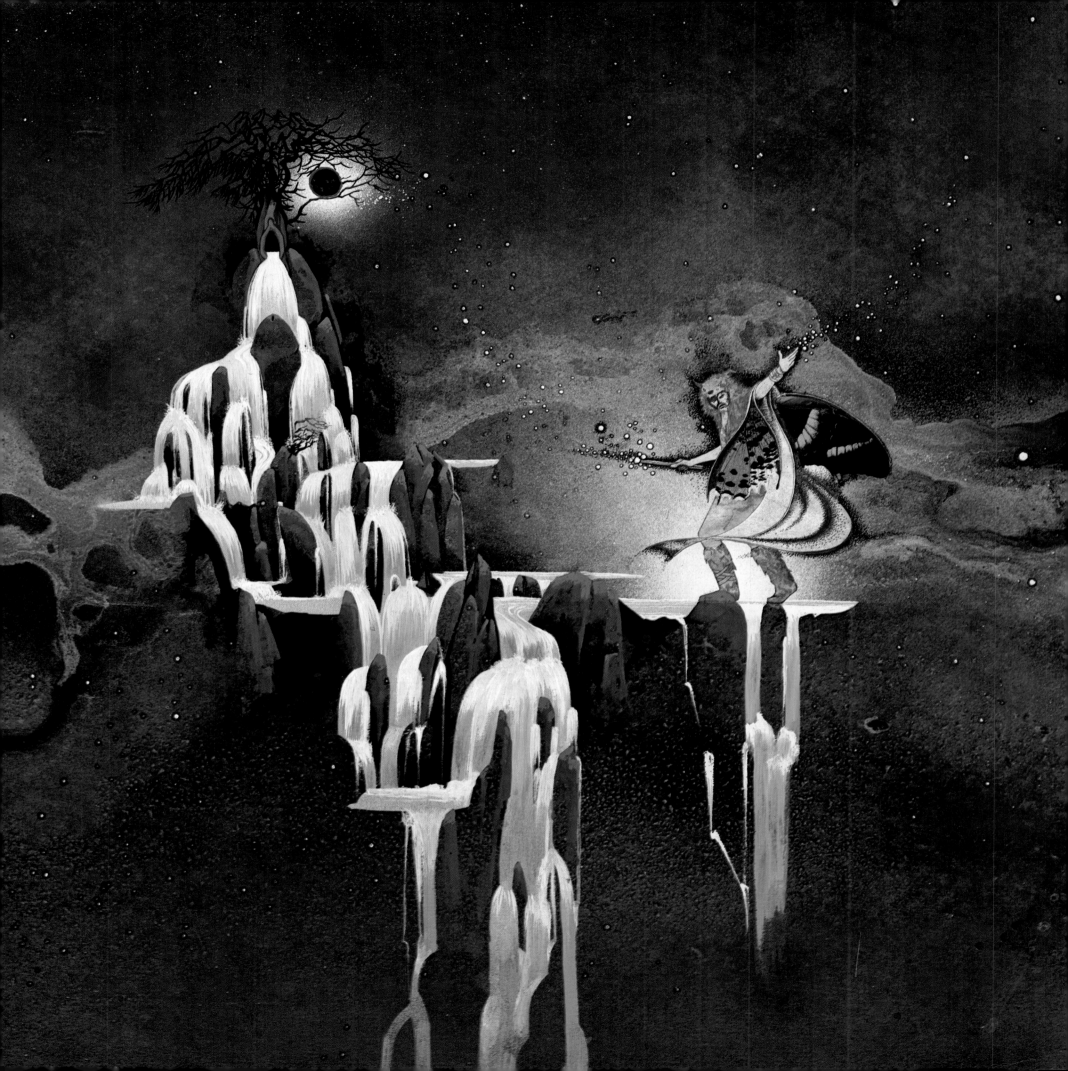

The drawing on page 73 was done as a new label for the Vertigo record company, and the company logo (which had been the old label) was slotted in beneath it. The crab and the orchid designs shown below were other drawings for record labels.

McKendree Spring Spring Suite

While finding a visual correlative for the idea of "spring," the drawing on pages 75 and 76 shows the links between an inner and an outer landscape. It was used for the cover of "Spring Suite," an album by McKendree Spring, and some of the preliminary sketches are shown on this page. Dean's first idea for the cover was to use a section of a melting ice palace. Later he decided not to show any signs of human life other than the pathways, and the figures which he had already drawn on them were covered over by ice forms. Dean says that only the slightest alteration was required to remove any hint of architecture, and have the melting palace revert back to an apparently natural form.

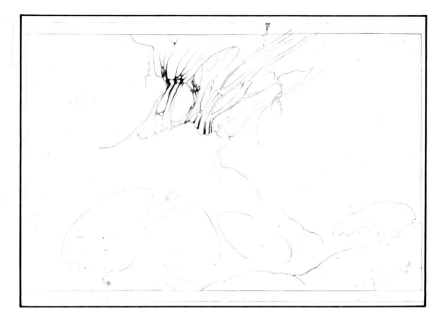

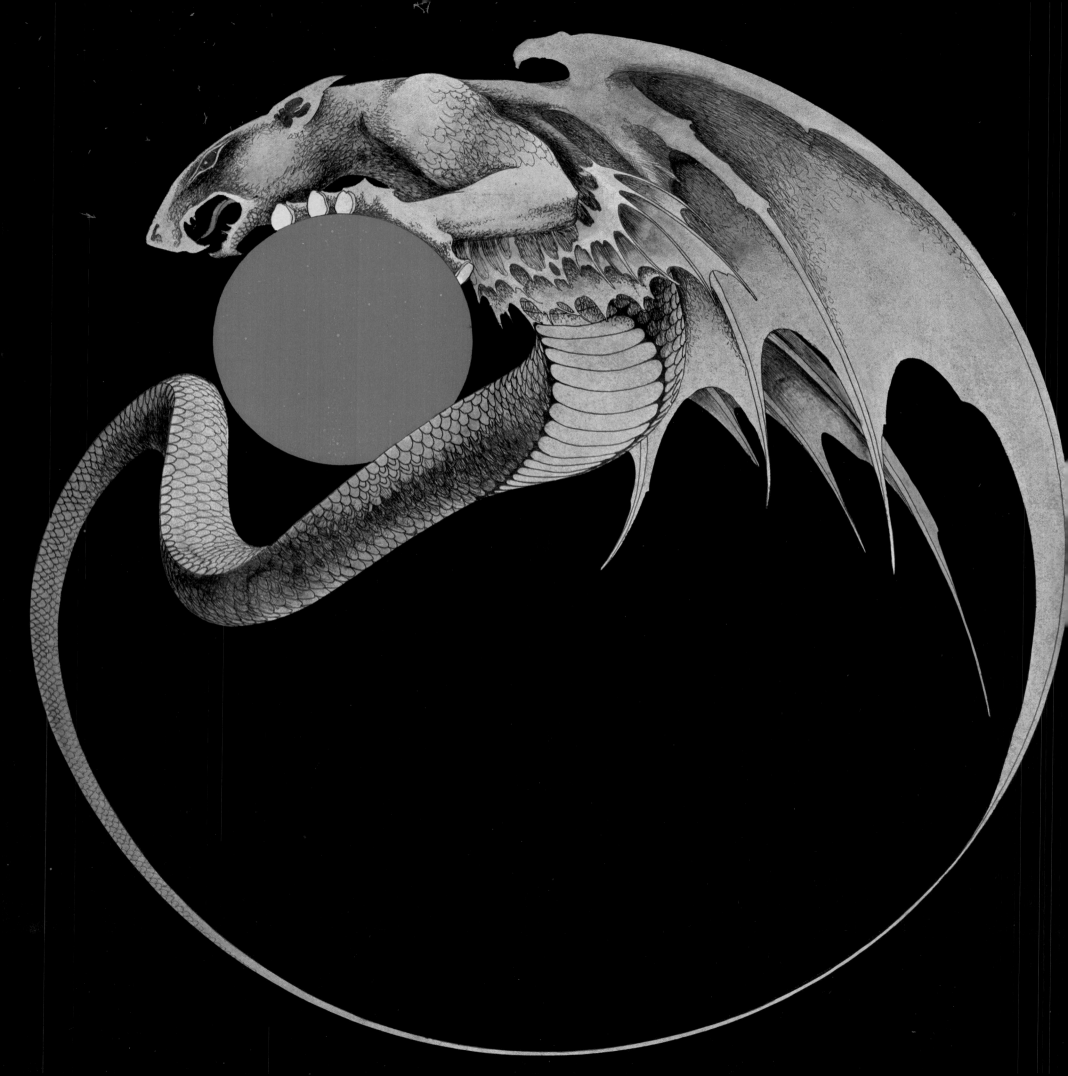

One of Dean's rare attempts to work in oils ("worse than painting with mud") led to this cover for SNAFU which, like the Ramases picture, opened up to tell a different, more complete, story. He bought himself a Teach-Yourself-Oil-Painting kit but found that although he liked the slipperiness of the paint, it was "a bit like floundering around in a swamp." While painting this picture he also worked on Bobby Harrison's (lead vocalist in SNAFU) solo album (pp. 77-78), which included a line photograph.

Roger Dean hand-wrote the label copy for all the records that Fly brought out as part of the total design. Fortunately there weren't very many as the label was only set up as a transitional measure. The green dragon on page 79 makes its first public appearance here.

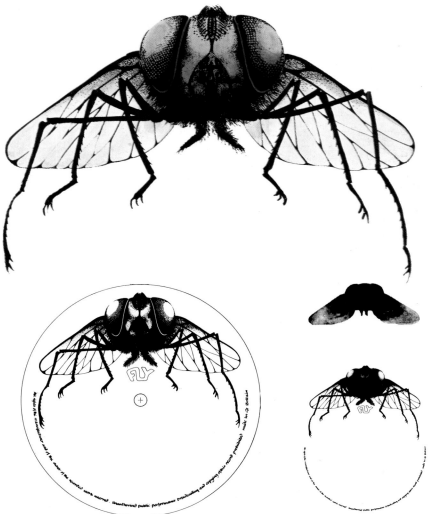

Figure 1 is Gollum. It was drawn at the suggestion of a friend. Figures 2-5 were done for Howard Brandy, who was producing horror movies at the time. They were posters which were not intended for the public but as part of a presentation package for the financial backers. Part of the brief was to depict the leading characters as Donald Pleasence and Christopher Lee, but as they had not yet agreed to be involved Dean was told not to make them look too realistic. Figure 6 was for the same film but this time Dean was asked to try it again with rats. Figure 7 is part of the press release material for "A Town called Bastard." Figure 8 is the cover for an American paperback edition of a book called "View over Atlantis" by John Michell. Dean had already read and liked the book, so when he was asked to do the cover, he agreed. The picture evokes a typically

3

4

8

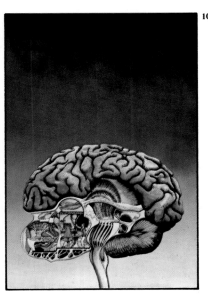

9

10

5

6

7

English countryside and is a view down an imaginary ley-line. He did two other book covers, for science-fiction paperbacks (figs. 9, 10). Dean designed about half a dozen film posters at this time (1971) but he decided that he did not like the style he had to work in, and soon stopped doing them.

The two following pages show the blue demon picture, done in 1972, and used in 1974 by Gravy Train.

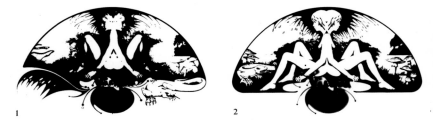

Dean was introduced to Virgin Records in 1970, soon after he started doing record covers. They asked him to do the label for their embryonic record company and their advertisements in the press. The mirror-image girl, who was to become their unofficial symbol, was firstly produced as a photograph (fig. 1). Dean then abandoned this, and went on to do a drawn version. This became the label (fig. 2) which was used in their first ads (figs. 3, 4). Dean used the mirror-image repeatedly for Virgin; often the pictures actually were mirror-images, but sometimes they only appeared to be.

All of the graphics were originally done in black and white. The first label (p. 87) to be used on a record was black and white, and it was not coloured until after the first few records came out. The label design combines a photograph and a drawing, a technique also used for Bobby Harrison's cover (pp. 77-78). The first graphics for the Virgin ads which appeared regularly in the music press only featured the Virgin label (fig. 2), since the

record company had not yet started producing records. After a few of these ads had appeared they decided they would like Dean to change the illustrated "Virgin" headings every other week or so. Rather than re-draw them from scratch, Dean saved time and maintained continuity by snipping the heading out of the newspaper and pasting it into a new drawing. He did this several times, and it is interesting to see how the images developed. The selection of graphics shown here is not comprehensive; it shows a range of his designs which were applied, among other things, to bags, T-shirts, and labels.

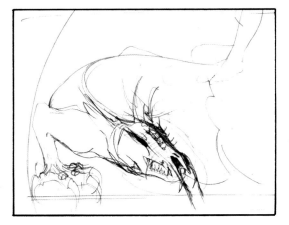

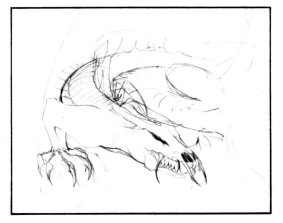

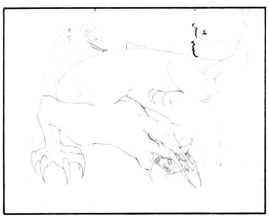

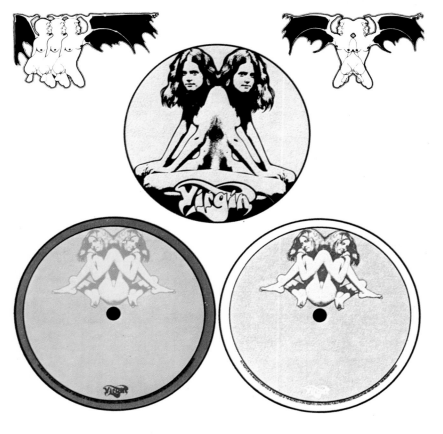

The pictures on the next page and on the following five pages were done for Greenslade. The series of drawings on page 88 shows Dean evolving his enigmatic magician. The multiple arms were retained from his indicision at the sketch stage, when he was trying to find the best position for a single arm. The first cover (pp. 89-90) was drawn almost twice the size it was to be reproduced, and it shows the "magician" in a giant cave, or natural auditorium. It was done on a board with enamel aerosols, and his use of the "marbling" technique was much more restrained and controlled than it had ever been before (for example, pp. 38, 39-40). He worked on the surface with inks and gouache and the figure was superimposed on this background. The title of the second Greenslade album (pp. 91-92), "Bedside Manners are Extra," was interpreted only in the figure of the magician, while the background evoked a late autumnal city scene. This is a rare instance of Dean's use of a style of architectural drawing foreign from his own, and it took him some time to resolve the massing of the buildings and the degree of detail in which he was going to draw them (p. 93). The wooden canopy around the figure, however, is much closer to Dean's own style. The original of this picture was actually destroyed in a fire before it was completely finished, but fortunately a transparency had already been made and this was used for the reproduction shown in this book.

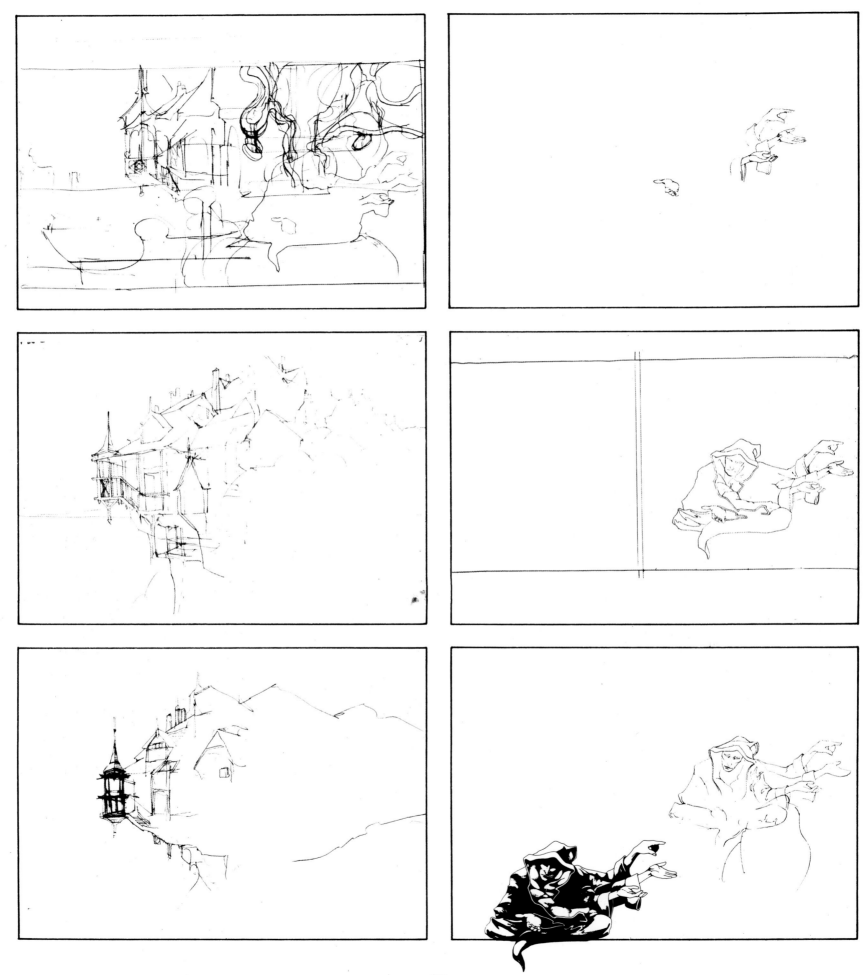

Badger

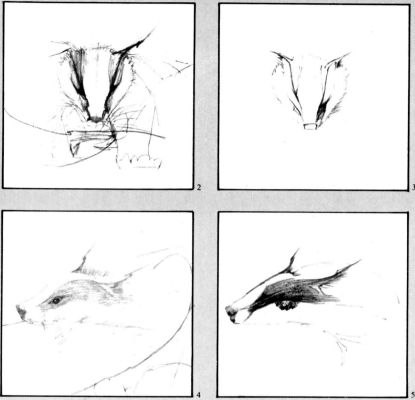

Roger Dean has always been an enthusiastic fan of badgers and he regrets that this is the only English mammal that he has not seen in its natural habitat. His long-standing fascination with badgers dates from when he came to England from Cyprus when he was nine and started drawing them in ink and in water-colour. The drawing on this page (fig. 1) was done when he was eleven or twelve. Later when Dean was designing his house (see pp. 132-144), he specified "badgers in the basement" among the wild life he would like to share it with.

Twenty years separate the early badger drawing from the others on this page, done for an album called "One Live Badger." Dean says that he remembered the early drawing as being almost identical to the later sketches, and that when his mother produced it years later, it came as something of a shock to find that it was actually very different. Dean felt that the first of the cover sketches (figs. 3 4) based on photographs of badgers, looked too innocent; he wanted to make them look wiser and fiercer (figs. 2, 5).

Badgers in the wild hibernate during the winter, so the animals shown on the Badger cover (pp. 95-96) are exhibiting unusual behaviour. As Dean says, "one feels they must have some ulterior motive for being out in such weather." Thus, for those familiar with the life-style of badgers, the image of badgers in the snow, in daylight, would be very surprising. Despite its simplicity this has been among Dean's most popular drawings. Here he has used only pencil and watercolour, applied directly on stretched cartridge paper; for him, an extremely restricted use of media. The drawing was done in about four hours.

The body of work Roger Dean has done for YES (from late 1971 onwards) includes some of his most widely-known projects to date. As a consequence of the group's popularity and their very large international album sales, the designs that Roger Dean has done for them have reached a larger audience than many of his other covers. His association with the group has given him the opportunity of sustaining and developing a set of ideas over a period of years and in a variety of media.

At the outset of Dean's working relationship with YES the sheer scale and scope of the work he was to do for and with the group could not have been anticipated. In retrospect the record covers and the stage designs, along with the programmes, badges, and other spin-off material seem to have been consciously designed to correspond with each other and with the music. This is surprising since the initial images were developed in isolation. Given Dean's interest in the synaesthetic interaction of the senses in the performing arts, he naturally took the opportunity of following through and realising these preoccupations when the time and the means to do so came his way, as he and Martyn worked on the YES stages. (He had envisaged a complete sound and light show on wheels as early as 1968. See pp. 43-44).

Roger Dean's own unique visual imagination undoubtedly conditioned the development of YES' public image. The themes of humanity's limitations in the face of limitless space, of great spans of time, and of the subjective nature of subjective impressions are, of course, not peculiar either to YES or to Dean. The combination of the two, however, seems to have been a singularly powerful and successful one, and it is the fact that a chord has been struck in the contemporary imagination that has enabled Dean to explore and enlarge the territory touched upon in the "Fragile" album cover.

Some time after YES' first album came out Dean met Phil Carson who runs Atlantic records in England. Carson wanted to introduce him to the group. The meeting did not finally take place until about two years and two albums later, just after "The Yes Album" was released. The band then went on an American tour, and when they returned Brian Lane, the group's manager, asked Dean to do the cover for their fourth album, which was to be called "Fragile." Dean recalls that this album cover was the hardest he had worked on up to that time, and he was by no means satisfied with the end result. The booklet inside was complicated because therewas to be a page for each member of the group

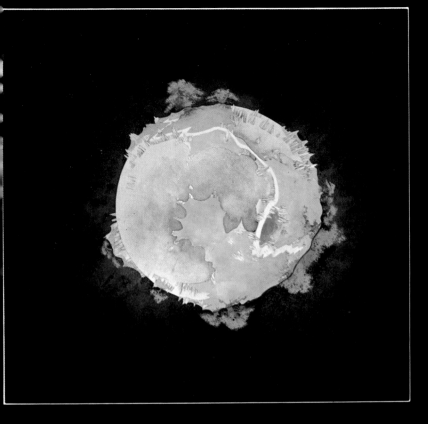

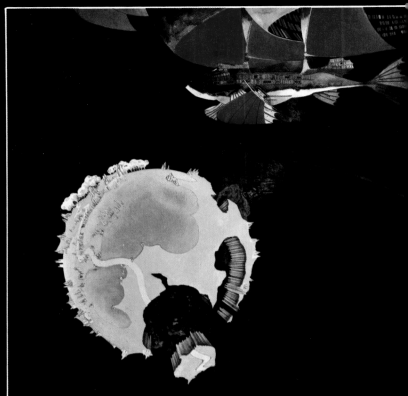

and it was a problem to balance the need to show their contrasting personalities with the need for a coherent design.

The cover presented even more difficulties. Dean's idea for it was a miniature world, while the group proposed the image of a fractured piece of porcelain. A compromise was effected; Dean drew the miniature world and then broke it. The two images on the "Fragile" cover were obviously related in time and although it was then considered complete in itself, the story was later followed through on the "Yessongs" album, and has since been developed into an as yet unpublished project.

The planet disintegrates but the inhabitants hav

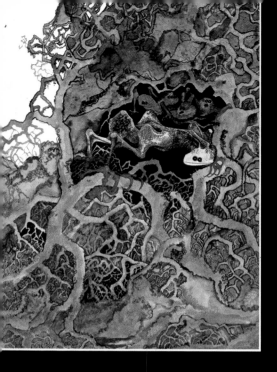

I would like to thank:– Rosaline Wakeman, Mr. & Mrs. C. Wakeman and complete family tree, Mrs. Symes, Mr. Herrera, the Atlantic Blues, the Concord Quartet, the Royal College of Music, The Strawbs and Roadies, David Katz, The Ronnie Smith Band, James Royal, A & M Records, The Music Press, Dan Wooding, David Bowie, Brian Lane, Lew Warbourton, Stanley Myers and all Session Mo's Tony Brainsby, Keith Goodwin, The Yes and Roadies, Annakata Music, Paramount, Screen Gems, All the London Recording Studios and Engineers, Essex Music, Toni Visconti, Gus Dudgeon, Jon Anthony, Eddie Offord, The Musical Bargain Centre, The Tony-Dee Showband, Dan Wooding, South Harrow Baptist Church, Wolfgang Amadeus Motzart, Arnold, Martin and Morrow, Sid Sat, Charlie Katz, All session Musicians, The White Bear Hounslow, The BBC, Colin Spiers, Roy Shea, Ex-members and Performers of Booze-Proof (White Hart Acton), Becky Arpold, Jon Schroeder, God Bless Brentford Football Club, Ken Scott, Piglet, the Top Rank Reading, The Woolfords, The Spinning Wheel, Roger Dean, Staff and Pupils of Drayton Manor County Grammar School and all my friends off and on the road too numerous to mention for helping to further my career either deliberately or by accident. P.S. One future offspring. Love to Everybody.

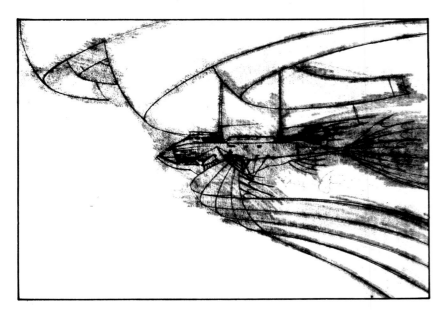

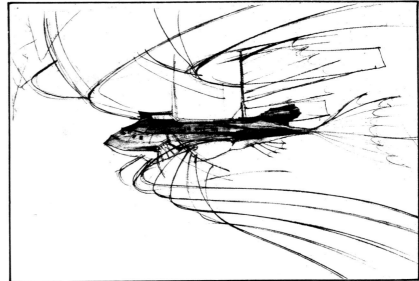

as spores through space. In the second picture on the "Yessongs" cover the spores impregnate a new planet (pp. 109-110), introducing life (pp. 111-112). In the fourth picture the cities evolve (pp. 113-114). Dean is concerned here with conveying a sequence of events which take place on a scale which we cannot wholly grasp; this is the material of myth. The idea of tracing a story through aeons of time occurs elsewhere in Dean's work (for example in the "Lighthouse" series pp. 32-34). The "Fragile" — "Yessongs" series is linked by a story, and this differs fundamentally from the "Lighthouse" series, which rings the changes on a single image.

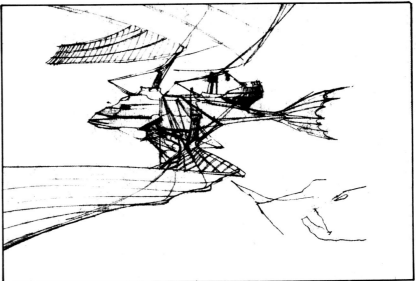

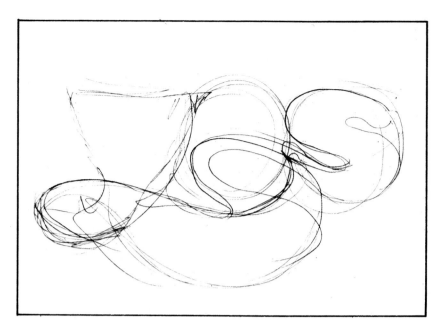
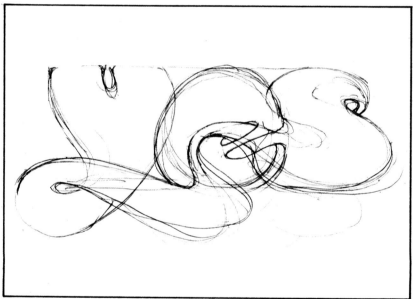
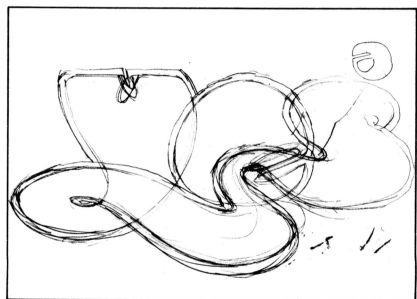
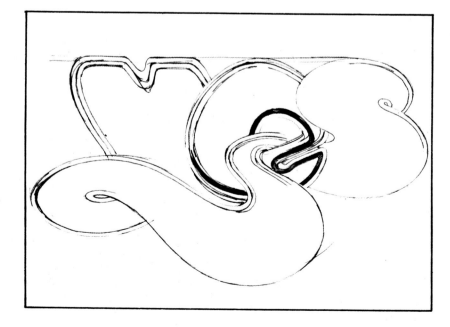

Close to the Edge

Roger Dean describes the drawing for "Close to the Edge" as being "another paradox miniature world" like the planet for "Fragile." Here the inspiration came directly from lakes and waterfalls seen and photographed on holiday in the Scottish Highlands as well as from photographs and descriptions of Angel Falls in Venezuela. Two years after the drawing was finished, quite by chance he came upon a similar phenomena in the Lake District: a small lake poised on the summit of a mountain. He says that he loves the idea of this picture but that he is not very satisfied with the result. He found it frustrating working with aerosol car enamel on such a small scale (24″ by 12″). Perhaps this is the one picture he would most like to do again. Ironically, in spite of this, it is the single picture that he has had most public response from.

Dean painted a related picture just afterwards which was to be used for promotion purposes for "Close to the Edge" (p. 104). It was only used once before it disappeared into the depths of Atlantic's files, but luckily it reappeared a year later. This very understated, almost monochrome work is one of the most beautiful of all of Roger Dean's pictures. It was during the course of his work on the "Close to the Edge" album that Dean first designed the YES logo (p. 103).

Between completing the two drawings for "Close to the Edge" and starting on "Yessongs" Dean bought himself an airbrush. The idea for the image on the cover of "Yessongs" was not conceived specifically as an album cover, and it was the first picture in which Dean used the airbrush. A problem which arose when he was spraying watercolour was that his cats walked all over the pictures and their prints showed up. Even when he tried to hide them with clouds they are still clearly visible (pp. 113-114). A Japanese magazine commented on the footprints in an article about Dean and speculated on whether his studio was frequented by roaming wild animals.

When YES came back from their American tour Dean showed them the "Yessongs" picture, which was to be the cover for a live album from their tours. He was disappointed to find that Jon Anderson and Brian Lane had their own ideas for the cover, a Holiday Inn matchbox. Eventually Dean's drawing was used, along with the three other pictures that make up the story already outlined above.

For reproduction on the album the full-size drawing (pp. 113-114) had two additions: the girl on the rock, and the spaceship. Dean didn't want these on the originals so he had them dropped in by the printers from separate drawings. Four of the six covers Roger Dean has done for YES have had such additions for various reasons. None of these additions appear in this book. The front cover graphics for "Yessongs" include a small version of the main drawing without additions.

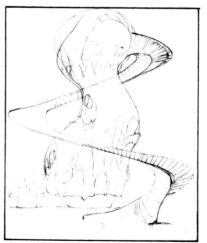

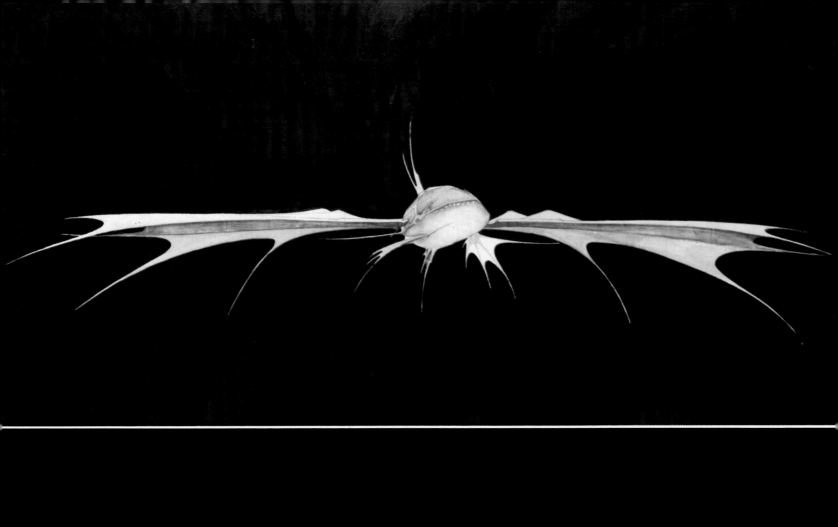

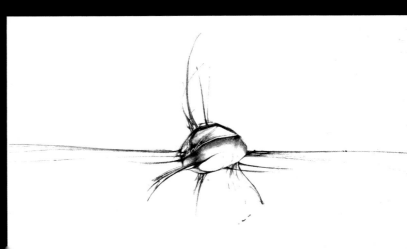

Roger Dean went to Japan with YES in March of 1973. During the course of the tour they discussed proposals for a stage and the designs for the cover of their forthcoming album "Tales from Topographic Oceans" Dean's original idea was that the design should work both as a drawing in its own right, and as a code for patterns located elsewhere. The final collection of landmarks was more complex than he had intended because it seemed appropriate to the nature of the project that everyone who wanted to contribute should do so. The landscape comprised, among other things, some famous English rocks taken from Dominy Hamilton's postcard collection. These are, specifically: Brimham Rocks, the Last Rocks at Lands End, the logan rock at Treen, and single stones from Avebury and Stonehenge. Jon Anderson wanted the Mayan temple at Chichen Itza with the sun behind it, and Alan White suggested using markings from the plains of Nazca. The result is a somewhat incongruous mixture, but effective nonetheless.

The drawing with the two blue children on it which was used for the back cover of "Yesterdays" (p. 120) had been done several years earlier. It was used on this cover because it was thought to have the mixture of nostalgia and déja-vu appropriate for an album of re-released early material. The picture of trees was designed to relate to this drawing, and included a girl from the English cover of "Time and a Word" (not done by Dean). The two drawings were intended to be used interchangeably as back and front covers.

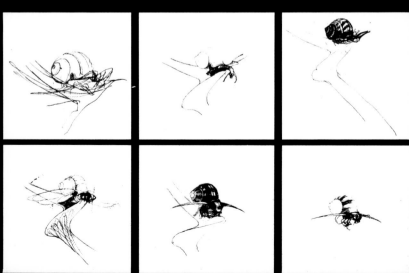

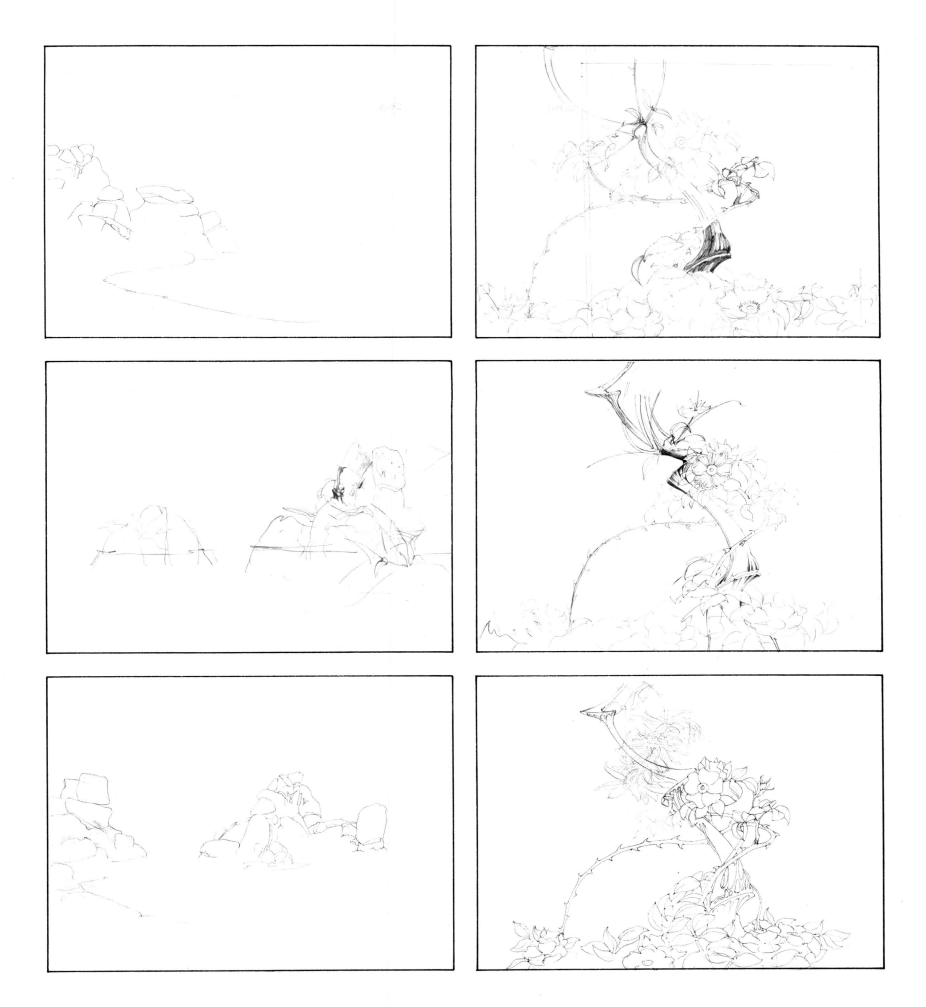

Relayer

The original drawing shown here on page 122 was done in 1966 and is one of the first in the RCA sketchbook. Dean once said that what he was striving for was to make his technique completely invisible so that the image could show through unimpaired. On being told that if that was what he was after he might just as well use a photograph, he quickly replied that this was exactly what he'd like to do: build it and then photograph it. If he could build his ideas he wouldn't have to draw them. As well as being his favourite YES cover, the "Relayer" album is the record of theirs Dean likes best. "My intention was to produce a giant

"gothic" cave. A sort of fortified city for military monks; a secret stronghold for a fantasy Knight's Templar."

The title "Happy Birthday" was given to the drawing on page 122 by Donald Lehmkuhl (to whom Dean has given it) and it is perhaps the only picture in the book with a real title. Lehmkuhl wrote the poem that appeared on the "Relayer" cover and also the text for the "Topographic Oceans" tour programme. The drawing was done for the inside of the "Relayer" album but was not used.

Roger Dean is often asked about the nature of the relationship between his pictures and the music. He says that he has very rarely heard the music before doing an album cover. "I cannot say that the music is ever a direct inspiration for my work. However, the music, the title, and the art work are all related, and must all affect each other to some degree. It's like the relation between a picture and its title. For example, if a picture was entitled "Peace" and the image was of a poppy field the significance would be different than if it was of a wrecked tank or a waterfall. The picture changes the title and the title changes the picture." Dean has not titled any of the pictures in this book but he is fascinated by the consequences of "naming" images. However he does not want an arbitrary title to interfere with the chain of associations the image evokes in each observer.

There is an unavoidable working relationship between the music and the images associated with it, and this tends to increase when the association is carried through over several albums. This has become most apparent in the work Dean has done with YES. The connection between music and visual imagery is much more flexible than that between words and pictures, since it has its basis in mood and atmosphere.

During the late 60's and early 70's some bands were working towards the idea of a concert being a total experience in which the emotional intensity of electronic music was enhanced by its combination with visual effects. The stage-sets that Roger Dean designed for YES with his brother Martyn allowed him to exploit the overlapping of visual and auditory sensations, and to try out the effect of a fantasy landscape in three dimensions. Roger Dean says "to consider that people come to concerts for music alone would imply a very

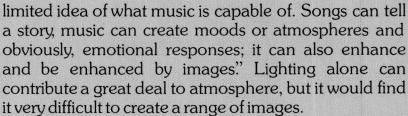

limited idea of what music is capable of. Songs can tell a story, music can create moods or atmospheres and obviously, emotional responses; it can also enhance and be enhanced by images." Lighting alone can contribute a great deal to atmosphere, but it would find it very difficult to create a range of images.

The stage for the "Topographic Oceans" tour was composed of ambiguous shapes that were meant to be transformed by the lighting, so that sometimes they appeared like flowers, sometimes like animals, or machines, or an inanimate landscape. The end result however, was severely compromised by the practical limitations of having 25 tons of equipment on tour and by the formalities of stage procedures.

The first stage used on the English tour to promote "Tales from Topographic Oceans" was incomplete; the sculptural forms (p. 125) were still only the patterns from which the moulds for the final stage were cast. Also, because of the smallness of British theatres, most audiences in this country only saw a fraction of the

shapes; there simply wasn't room to get them all on the stage. The castings for the final version which was used on the 1974 American tour were made of thin translucent walled fibreglass and lit inside and out (pp. 126-127).

The stage was a joint design by Martyn and Roger Dean in that they agreed on a basic approach and then separately designed the ingredients. Martyn designed and built the drum rostrum (p. 126) that was the centre of the stage and Roger designed the doorway, the backcloth and the organ pipes. Both these first two stages were built in Clive Richardson's studio and he modified the sets when Rick Wakeman left the group and Patrick Moraz joined.

The latest stage set used by YES for their 1975 American tour was designed by Martyn Dean (with the exception of the backcloth) and built by him and Clive Richardson. The backcloth was made by Felicity Youett to Roger Dean's design, as was the previous one. She is shown assembling it on page 128.

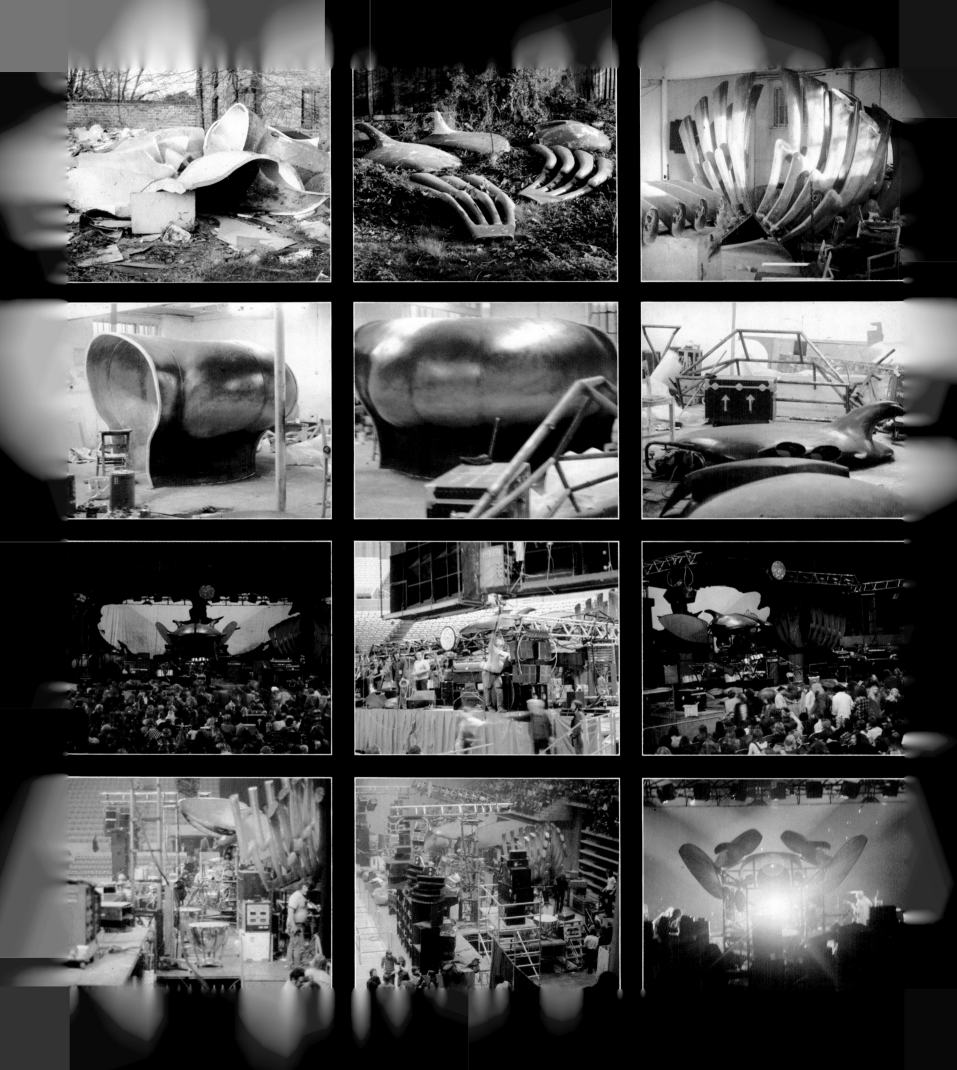

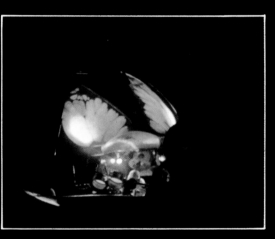

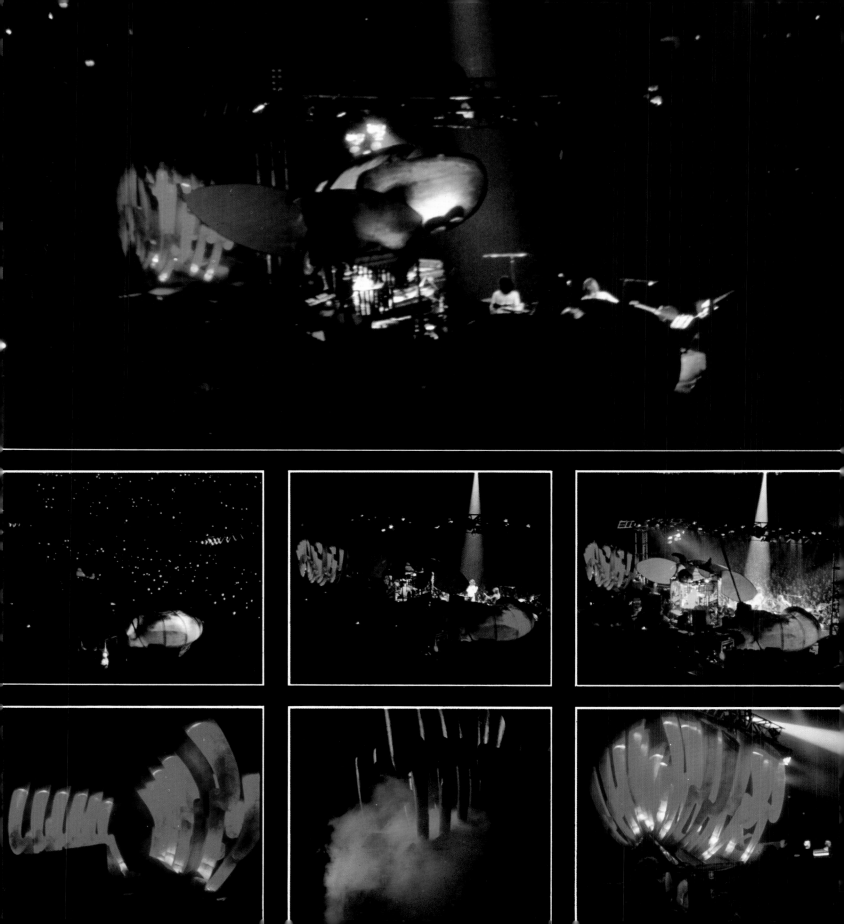

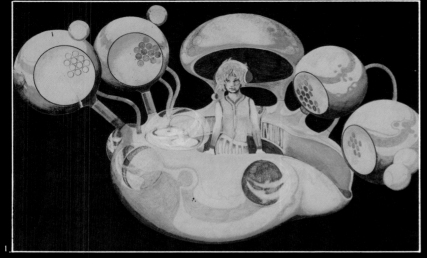

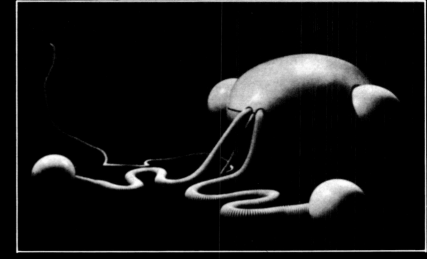

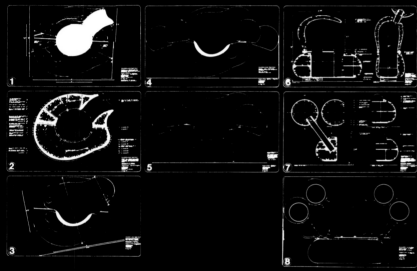

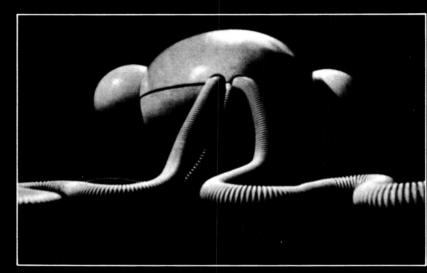

Roger and Martyn Dean have worked on several projects together aside from the stage designs. In most cases they each designed separate units within a jointly conceived framework. For example, within the category of animal-like children's furniture which they entered in the Maples-Telegraph exhibition (see p.16), Martyn designed a foam dinosaur and Roger did his "Teddy Bear" chair. The "portable record shop" (p.129 figs. 1 and 2) was the only object on which Martyn and Roger collaborated on the design, the structure, and the drawings and they both now feel that it was a mistake.

Martyn first started work on his "Retreat Pod" while he was still at the Central School of Art, although it was

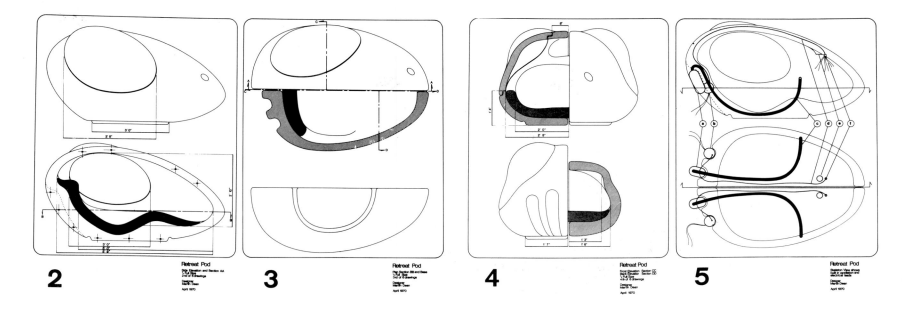

2

3

4

5

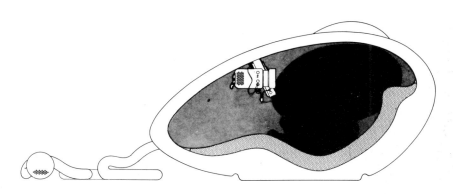

not a college project. The first design was meant to accommodate two or three people (p. 129 figs. 3, 4, 5). One of the things that interested Martyn at the time was the difference in the perception of volume when an object was seen from the outside and when it was experienced from the inside. He experimented with the effects of control on perceived internal space, utilising such means as sensory deprivation and, at the other extreme, a situation of massive audio-visual stimulation. The drawings on page 130 and the photographs on page 131 are of a pod which was smaller than the first version, but whose design was much more sophisticated and adaptable. It was constructed out of a series of clear plastic bubbles which were blown

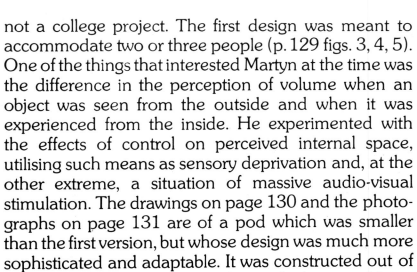

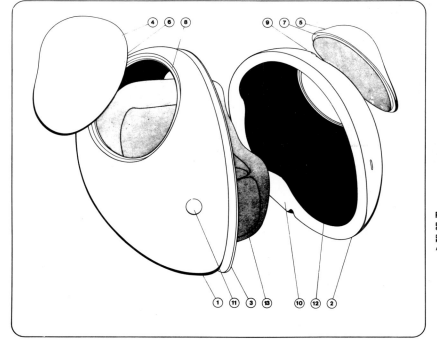

6

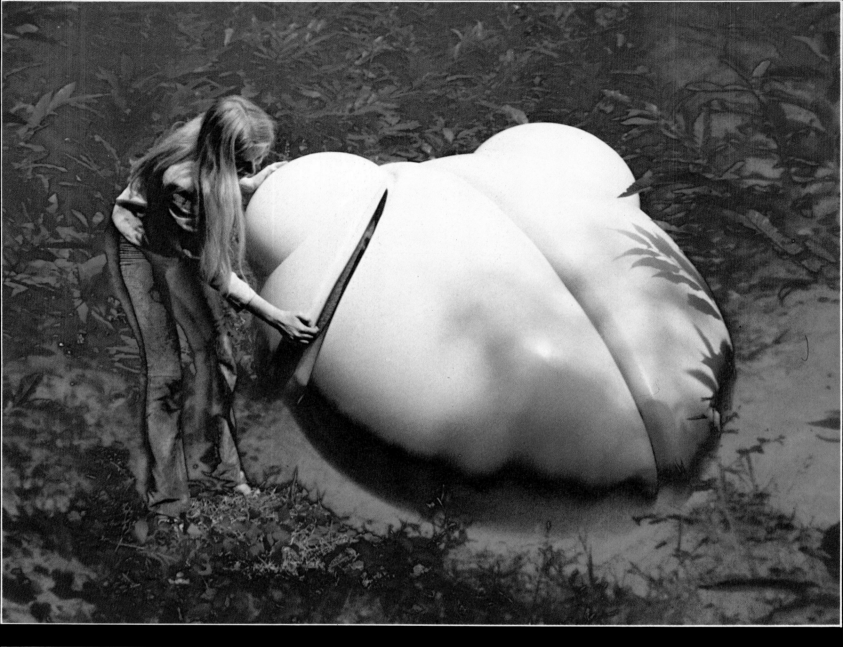

through templates. These were then lined with rigid foam, and finally upholstered. The speaker bubbles contained 10-inch speakers, and for the Maples-Telegraph exhibition, where it made its first appearance, it was packed full of audio-visual equipment, perhaps not entirely to Martyn's liking. Soon after this, half of the pod made a brief appearance in Kubrick's "Clockwork Orange." Whilst Martyn Dean was constructing his "Retreat Pod," Roger did some drawings of how he thought it would turn out, and one of these is shown on page 133, figure 4.

In every word we speak there lies a meaning sleeping, voiceless in its repose. These words, these meanings once were rough-hewn. Raw. Puissant. Their sounds were awesome invocations vibrating directly upon the resonating thought and feeling of those who uttered and heard them. The sound, the thought, the feeling were one with meaning. But time and custom, use and abuse have smoothed our words like pebbles tossed in millennia of surf. This word, that word, every word assumes a habitual shape, a featureless form that signals object or action but rarely thought or feelings. Original diamond becomes a pill of glass.

Such a word is *house.* What, then, is a house?

It is everything it means.

In its misty Sanskrit origin, *house* descends from two related words with cognate sounds: *skauti,* he covers or hides; and *kuhara,* a house. Disseminated by interminable wandering, translated by millions of tongues over thousands of years, these two sounds passed into most of the languages of Europe and near Asia: in Old Persian, we have *keuto* (hide); in Greek, *kutos* (a hollow vessel); in Latin, *scutum* (a shield); in Serbian, *kŭca* (a house); in German *Haut* (hide) and *Haus* (house), and so on. In modern English they gave rise to many significant words: *house,* of course, and obviously *hut,* but also *husband, hussy, husk, husting, huddle,* as well as *to hide* and *hide,* the pelt of a beast. At the core of them all is the principle of protection, refuge and concealment. Remember: very early houses were probably poles upon which were stretched animal skins. Early military shields were certainly made of hide.

A house, then, is a shield, a hide, a shelter against the hostilities of man and nature. In a house one remains hidden, secured by a skin tougher than one's own. A house is the barrier between man and peril, just as his epidermis is a barrier between man and bacteria. It is the magic circle in which fears are laid to rest. A house is an extension of human physical reality itself, another skin, a thicker hide.

Donald Lehmkuhl 1975

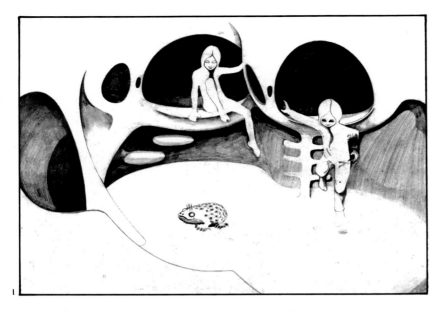

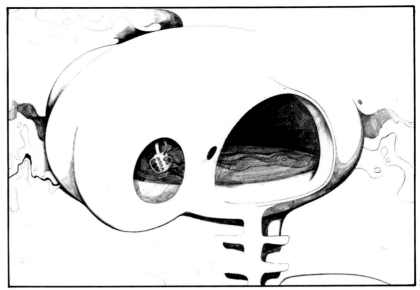

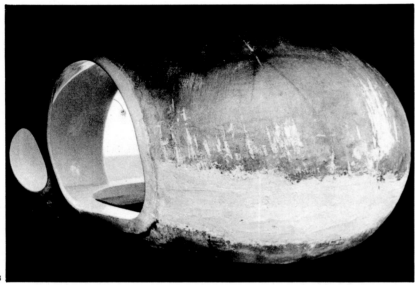

Working in the school of furniture design at the Royal College of Art, Roger Dean was struck by the extent to which furniture was made to compensate for inadequate architecture. He also felt that both of these design areas, domestic architecture and furniture, were based on assumptions that missed out some of the essential requirements of a human dwelling place. From thinking about problems related to furniture's role within architecture, Dean found himself questioning the very nature of domestic architecture, and the role of the house itself.

"The role of the home is to provide security and privacy. All else follows from this." Roger Dean started from this premise and built a house around it. "Privacy is not just being alone. Its most important aspect is choice. One must be able to control the extent and advent of any intrusion. This applies on both an indivi-

dual and a "family" level. Each individual should ideally have somewhere to go which is completely their own domain. It would be independently and physically fully controllable (access, temperature, lights, sound, etc.). Almost a home within a home. This private place may or may not include the sleeping area, but if it does not, then the sleeping area should itself contain these control features."

"Security is a much more complex concept. It extends from areas of civil liberties and legal rights, which cannot be gone into here, to the more intangible areas of psychological security: the defendable-castle concept. A home, besides needing security, needs something to be secure from. It requires a contrast from its domesticity, something as elemental as a thunderstorm perhaps, to enhance the feelings of security" (see page 138).

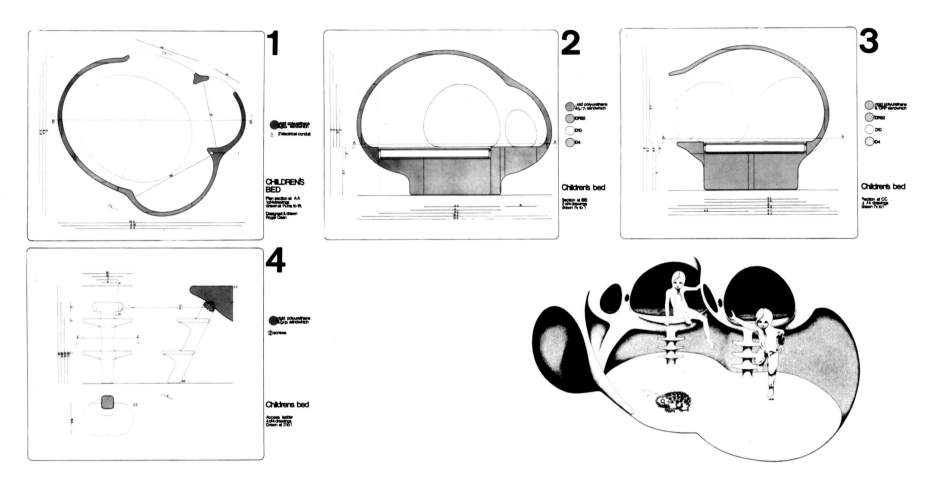

1

CHILDREN'S
BED

Plan section at AA
full size drawings
drawn 1¾ ins. to 1ft.

Designed & drawn
Roger Dean

2

Children's bed

Section at BB
2 of 4 drawings
drawn 1¾ to 1

3

Children's bed

Section at CC
3 of 4 drawings
drawn 1¾ to 1

4

Children's bed

Access ladder
4 of 4 drawings
Drawn at 3 to 1

"Within the home there are different areas of activity where these basic requirements predominate. The architecture of these areas should enhance and reflect the satisfaction of these requirements and of the particular activity taking place. In many cases the relationship of the different parts of the room or area is of such crucial importance to the roles of the room, both physical and especially emotional, that its success or failure is probably already decided before the furniture and fittings that traditionally define and symbolize the activities of the room are added."

In other words: an empty box is traditionally "made" into a dining-room or bedroom by the addition of six chairs and a table, or a bed. Dean's intention is to demonstrate that this is often an inadequate definition of a room.

Roger Dean's first project to be based on these considerations was in his design for a sleeping area, where he feels they are most important. He started work on his bed after he designed the "Sea Urchin" chair, while he was still at the RCA. Early on he felt that the problem of making the ideal place to sleep could

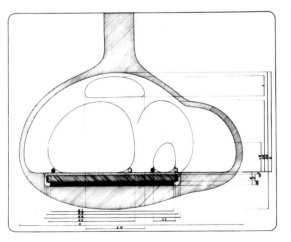

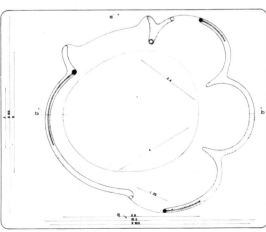

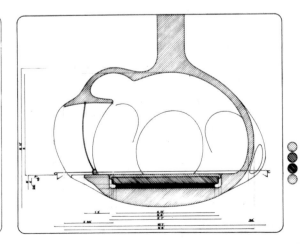

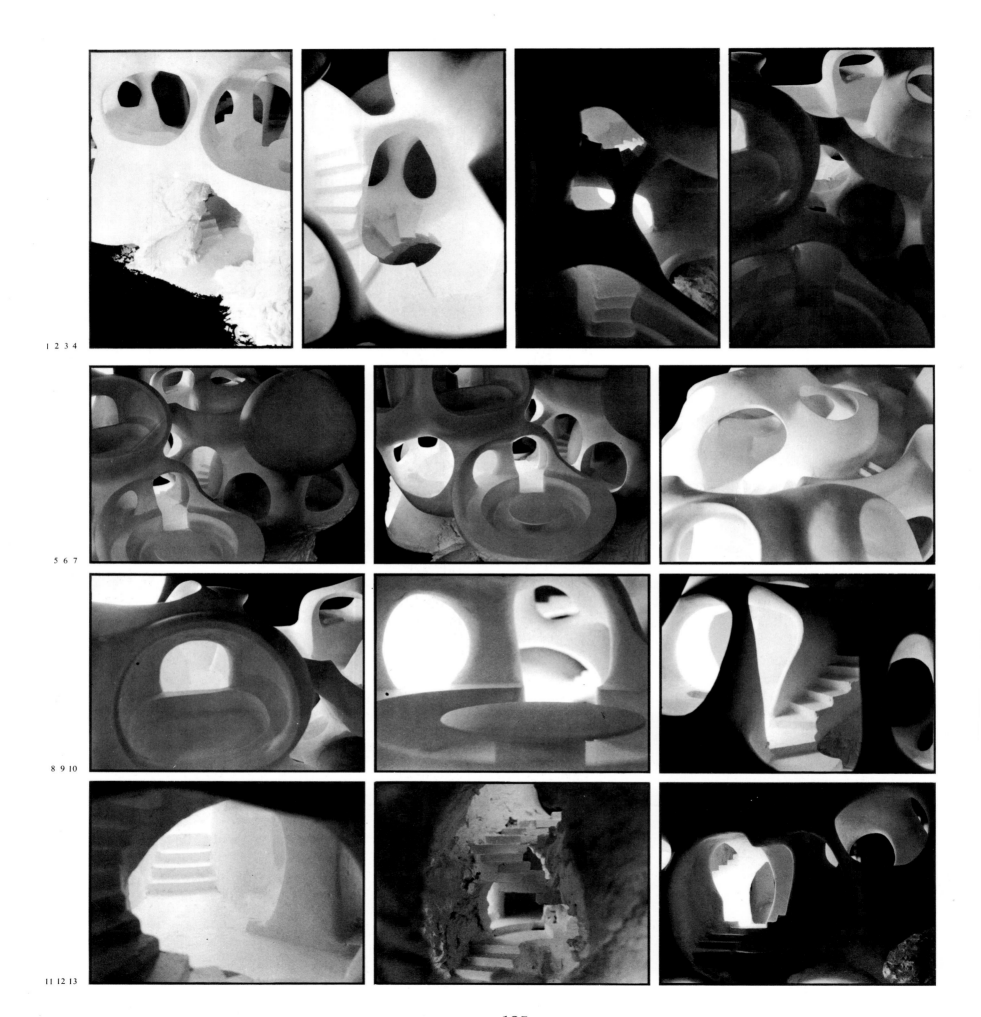

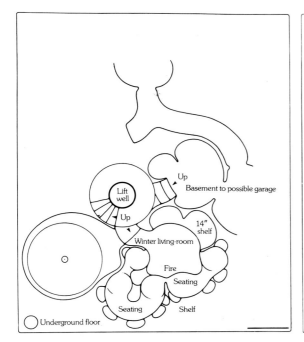

Lift well
Up
Up
Basement to possible garage
14" shelf
Winter living-room
Fire
Seating
Seating
Seating
Shelf

○ Underground floor

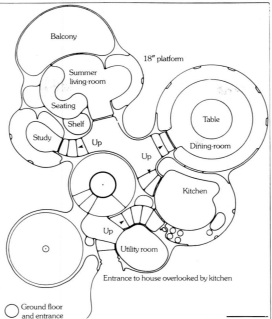

Balcony
18" platform
Summer living-room
Seating
Shelf
Study
Up
Table
Dining-room
Up
Kitchen
Up
Utility room
Entrance to house overlooked by kitchen

○ Ground floor and entrance

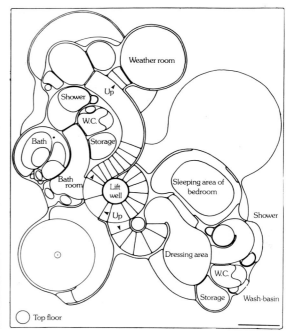

Weather room
Shower
Up
W.C.
Bath
Storage
Bath room
Lift well
Sleeping area of bedroom
Shower
Up
Dressing area
W.C.
Storage
Wash-basin

○ Top floor

not be solved simply by designing a comfortable platform. "With all the data available I felt one should be able to take the technology of a healthy comfortable mattress more or less for granted. What was crucial was the placing of that mattress in space."

He began by thinking in terms of his own emotional reactions to space, and by investigating areas which might cause anxiety. Prior to building the first prototype he made many drawings and models. The first prototype he built was of the smallest and least complicated sleeping unit (fig. 3 p. 133). He had been informally testing his ideas on people, and when this first prototype had actually been made it was possible to try them out for the first time. He found that it received an enthusiastic reaction from people of varying ages and backgrounds, and he interpreted this as a positive response ·to the enhancement of their sense of security. He found that many children and some adults were anxious about hidden spaces under the bed or behind full-length curtains, and that unknown recessed areas, wardrobes, hanging clothes, etc. are often construed as being potentially threatening.

Dean discovered that people's instinctive responses varied only in intensity or in orientation: while some would feel midly uncomfortable in a bedroom which had all the disquieting features he had found, others would be so disturbed as to be quite unable to sleep. Talking to people confirmed his own thoughts that the problem could be solved in terms of strategy. The possibility of unknown, hidden presences within the room, and the difficulty of one's relation to people coming into the room, especially those who did not habitually share it, revealed themselves to be very real problems and outweighed considerations of the size of the bed, the softness of the mattress, or the number of pillows.

Dean was beginning to conceive of an environment as a total ambience which would provide a complement to the intangible needs experienced by people in a given situation. He found that it was the space itself that needed alteration to help people to relax; certain features tended to inhibit relaxation and to foster anxiety, which would have its effect on people's ability to sleep easily. The "womb-like" shape of the bed was not a design concept imposed from without but a consequence of answering certain strategic requirements for a bed within a specially designed house.

Roger Dean specified these requirements as follows: In the dark, kneeling in the sleeping space, one should be able to feel the whole space by stretching out one's arms. From the inside, kneeling at the entrance to the bed, with one hand either side of the entrance, one should totally dominate access to the sleeping area. From a lying position in the bed one should be able to see the whole room, especially the entrance. The bed should be high enough off the ground (at least four feet) so that even when lying down one is not lower than, and therefore in an inferior relation to, anyone else in the room. Ideally the entrance to the room should be below floor level. If there is a window to the outside from the bed this should be small (maximum two feet by three feet) and should have sufficient

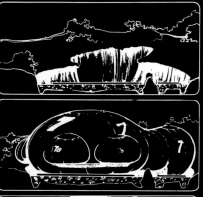
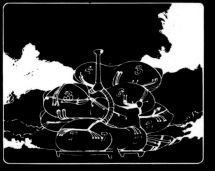

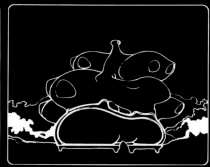

elevation not to be overlooked by anyone outside.

The first models that Dean made were for a whole bedroom, while later ones were for a "bed" conceived as a unit. The most important characteristic of his design in its final form was that it was halfway between a bed and a bedroom. The drawings on page 134 show designs for two such beds that could be manufactured as individual objects, but would then have to be integrated with their architectural setting. Figure 3 on page 133 is a photograph of the only prototype that was built, the children's bed being the most practicable for experiment and exhibition purposes. Dean feels that it would be unwise to actually build something this small into a house, and that all beds should be of a size to comfortably accommodate two adults.

The full-size bed (bottom of p.134) has a ledge all round it so that the wall does not come down to the mattress. This counteracts any uncomfortable feeling which might be caused by the closeness of the walls (their curvature and lack of surface detail minimizes their presence). This is particularly important around the head end which has three deep bays. These bays provide extra space around the head as well as storage space for books, and control of light and heat for the whole room.

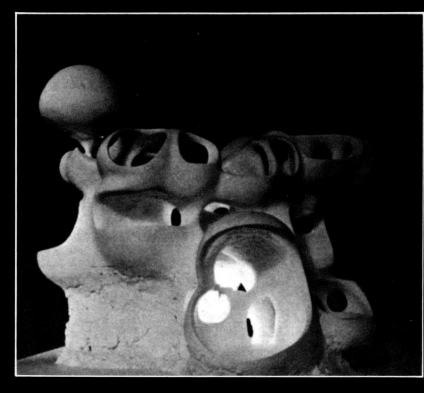

Having made the bedroom an extension of the bed, the obvious next step was to investigate the application of a similar approach to the design of the whole house. As has already been stressed, the major role of the house is to provide privacy and security. The bedroom,

137

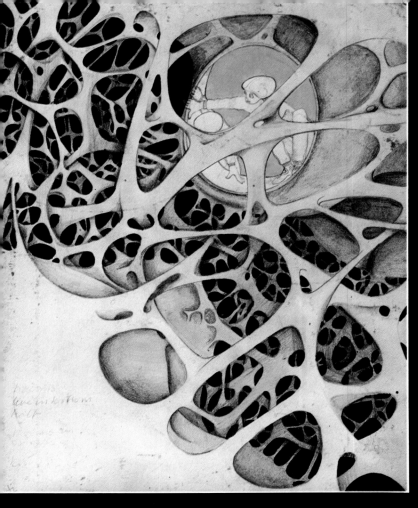

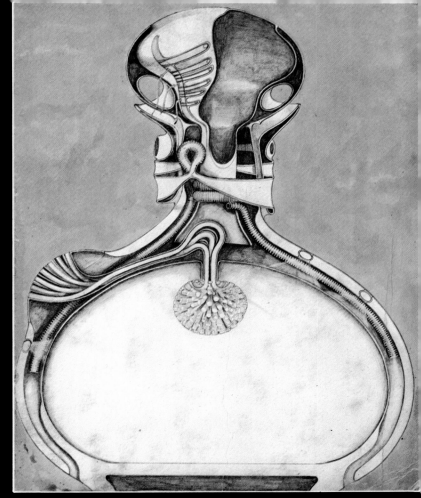

as we have seen, is the one room in which these considerations are most essential; in other rooms their emphasis is modified according to their function as living areas. For example, the bathroom, while apparently demanding a similar approach to privacy and security, can be seen on closer examination to be more dependent on cultural conceptions of modesty and dignity.

Areas to be used for every day communal activities invoke a less critical but more complex set of criteria, since they need to accommodate varying numbers of people engaged in various activities, both social and private. In the kitchen, in contrast to the bedroom and the bathroom, social activity takes precedence over a passive or vulnerable state, and the importance of the purely functional considerations of ergonomics is increased proportionately. The cooking area adjoins an amenity room containing laundry and storage facilities,

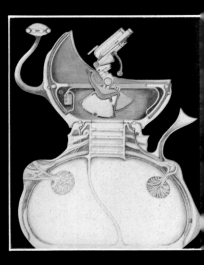

As well as being a place efficiently equipped for the preparation of food and other household chores, the kitchen is a congenial place for informal meals and gatherings. Since someone working in the kitchen may well be alone in the house possible anxiety is reduced

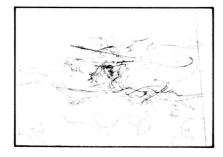

by the dominant position of the kitchen in relation to the rest of the house. The amenity area which it overlooks may also provide a safe play area for very young children. This part of the house was designed to be extremely flexible, since it has to provide for a variety of interrelating practical and social situations. In many homes, the kitchen does become the heart of the house.

The dining room, to which it is connected, is designed for a much more specific purpose: here people meet to eat together. Most human societies attach a certain degree of ceremony to the sharing of food and it seems to have an implicit ritualistic significance. To enable people to appreciate the food and each other's company fully, distractions both visible and audible are minimized, and they sit around a round table, which easily accommodates varying numbers of people.

The basic problems in the interaction of people in the living area is discussed in some detail on pages 18, 19, and 20 in relation to landscape seating.

Roger Dean thinks that two distinct emotional moods are associated with the living room, and in order to provide for the full development of both of these he has designed two separate areas, metaphorically called the "winter living room" and the "summer living room." Even in climates where the seasonal contrasts are not dramatic, the terms convey the difference in atmosphere.

The winter living room is conceived of as a cosy refuge for winter evenings from the cold and storms going on outside. It is below ground level, and the lack of windows simplifies the layout of the room and limits the number of access points, while emphasising the feeling of a snug enclosure. The focal point of the room is the fireplace. An open fire is essential to the mood of the winter living room. Its value is not simply as a source of heat, but it also has "a primeval emotional role to play."

Figure 3 on page 19 shows the winter living room. The various seating areas are arranged to maintain a sense of emotional security, for example by putting the door in view, forwards of all seating.

The summer living room, while fulfilling the same strategic requirements in adapting itself to a similar complex of roles, is very different in its essential feeling. It is designed to admit the maximum of light and to play down the contrast between inside and outside. A transparent partition separates the room from a veranda or balcony, and even on days when this had to be closed, the dividing line between them would remain ambiguous. This impression would be increased by plenty of plant life, indoors and out.

Corridors and staircases, as well as providing an important physical link between the rooms, have a further role in being part of what Roger Dean calls the "accidental space." "The purpose of this accidental space is to literally compound complexity and intricacy so that the house is not known at once. It gives scope for exploration and gradual knowledge; a factor which complements feelings of privacy." These are areas within the house which have no specific function, and include attics and cellars, and the gaps between rooms. Dean likes the idea of such mysterious spaces being shared by other creatures; he has expressed his pre-

ment in its own right, and is also equipped to relay and exaggerate certain information about the outside world to other parts of the house. Dean sees it as being especially applicable to the winter living room, where the effect of introducing the sound of howling winds and other primeval elements into an enclosed, protected space is similar to that of the open fire (or the telling of ghost stories). The sounds of wind and rain are controlled as they play on a series of instruments: it is a form of Aeolian harp. This can produce some eerie sounds. Within the weather room the sun's rays play on various lenses and prisms and are split up into a constantly changing "light show."

The photographs on page 135 show a one-twelfth scale model of the house which Roger Dean made while he was at the RCA. This was built to show the internal spaces and their interrelationship and it has whole sections of wall cut away to allow one to see inside. (An idea of the possible architectural form of the exterior is given on page 150.) The model was conceived as a three-dimensional "plan" connected by staircases. The plans on paper were also drawn one-twelfth actual size and are shown (much reduced) on

ference for owls and ravens nesting in the attic and badgers in the basement. This would help to blur the boundaries between the man-made structure and its natural setting (fig. 1 p. 138).

To provide such a link in another way is the function of the "weather room." (fig. 2 p. 138). It is intended as a means of accentuating at will the contrast between the domestic security of the home and the unpredictability of the elements raging outside. It is used in two different ways: it is an observation turret and a place of entertain-

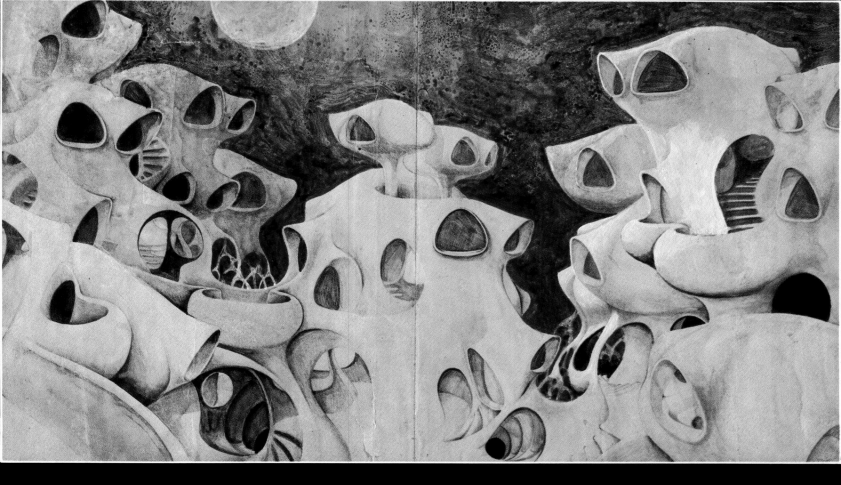

page 136. Figure 6 on page 137 is a photograph of the model under construction showing the plaster walls being added to the floors.

Figures 1 to 5 on page 137 show the proposed method of construction of the house using pneumatic moulds and a concrete and foam layered coat.
1. Excavation and laying of foundations. 2. The moulds are placed and then inflated. 3. Stairways and floors are fixed in space, window and door moulds added. 4. Plumbing and electrical circuits are fixed. 5. A first skin of fire-resistant glass fibre or concrete is sprayed on, then a layer of polyurethane foam, followed by an outer layer of concrete. The moulds are then removed.

While working on the designs for the house, Roger Dean was also envisaging ways in which such architectural forms could be used for communal living. The drawing of an interior "landscape" on page 20 is one of these. The drawings reproduced on the next few pages gives an idea of the possible exterior appearance of such dwelling complexes.

The Green Castle picture (p. 140) was done as part of a series of drawings for a story project which was abandoned. They all featured a dragon and its rider,

for which the sketches are shown on page 139. (See also pages 145-150.) Dean imagined the dragon-rider on an epic journey which, as elsewhere in his work, he used as a pretext for including details of his architectural schemes.

In the RCA sketchbook are a number of early drawings for village and small town scale projects. Because of the sociological and psychological ideas discovered by his work on the house, it was a logical extension to apply these to communities. Dean explored the possibilities of houses on stilts, tree-houses, cave-villages, walled towns and castles etc. There are countless precedents for such architectural forms, starting with the most ancient types of human habitation (as well as those of animals and birds) and they have never ceased to exert a strong hold on the imagination. A unique quality of Dean's design method is his application of the advantages of modern technology to such fundamental or "archetypal" concepts. He continues to study these and to try to isolate the elements of these recurrent ideas, in order to utilise them to greater advantages in his own work.

The houses on stilts (pp. 139 and 141) were con-

142

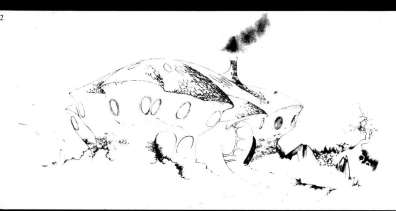

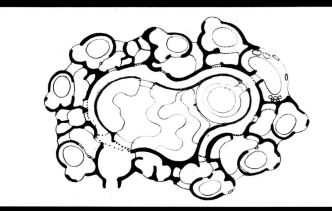

ceived as being surrounded by water, which might be swamp or sea. The city in the background on pages 113 and 114 is another example of a city elevated above water.

In the early drawings on pages 141 and 142, Dean had not resolved the problem of drawing windows. He had made them cavernous, neglecting to include glass, lights or people, and these window shapes, rather like those of eye-sockets in a skull, have a rather foreboding effect. Although Dean now describes this as a mistake (which it certainly was in design terms), there s no doubt that at this stage he relished the inclusion of

elements of Gothic horror in his drawings. In the drawing on page 142 the design of the windows has been improved and the overall impression is much less oppressive. This drawing was done to show the inter-relationship of structural units, and Dean's fascination with communicating stairways, pathways and balconies is apparent here. The drawing with the toads in the lift was a lighthearted sketch for a rural village (p. 143). It became the basis for the later designs on pages 147-150.

Figures 2 and 3 on page 143, and the drawings on page 144 differ from the preceding ones as they were

for two projects that were commissioned and were actually intended to be built. Unfortunately they have not gone beyond the design stage so far. They are designs for a building for Virgin Records' studios, which was to provide additional accommodation. It comprises eight bedrooms, a communal kitchen dining room and a central living area. It was to be clad in Cotswold stone so as to blend into the surroundings, and would have been in separate grounds, out of sight from the old manor house and its outbuildings.

Page 144 shows the two parts of a design for a playground in a children's hospital in South London.

The building contains swings, a helter-skelter, and a network of small rooms to climb into. The interior was to be very intricate so as to give plenty of scope for exploration. The second part of the project was the transformation of a piece of flat land into a landscape including pathways, small hills, tunnels and bridges. The main pathway winding through the whole landscape was to be wide enough for nurses to push wheelchairs along, and the smaller ones were for children on foot. The whole site was surrounded by the children's wards so that the view from the windows could also provide visual entertainment.

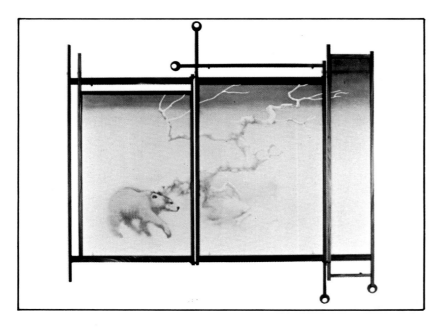

The frame for this screen was designed and built by Richard La-Trobe Bateman, and painted by Roger Dean for use in the front window of Steve Howe's health food shop "Brownies."

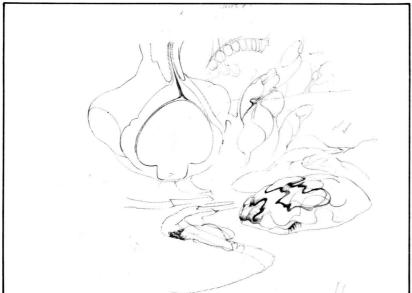

The last picture in this book is also the most recent of Roger Dean's record covers, which have been appearing increasingly infrequently during the last couple of years. It was done during the period when this book was being completed, for Steve Howe's first solo album, "Beginnings." Here once again we see Dean's preoccupation with the integration of "architecture" into a landscape. Steve Howe originally wanted an image in which the relationship between the interior and exterior was ambiguous. It was done with a specific place in mind, the coastal area north of Lochinver in Scotland, where the uneven rocky ground is broken up into tiny islands in sea lochs and small inland lakes, all of which interpenetrate each other.

This represents one aspect of the world that Roger Dean loves, a world undisfigured by the hand of man, in which he may find images that correspond with the stages of his own inner life. The depredations wrought in the name of human progress by large-scale agriculture and urban development are antithetical to Dean's vision. He shows us glimpses of an alternative system of living in which human existence blends in with that of the rest of nature. This vision of his seems immediately familiar and plausible, in that it touches innate memories, and also points to a future which is not the nightmare we dread, and yet which we can recognise as being imminent in the present. Dean's optimism links what we instinctively value in the past with the positive potential of twentieth-century technological advancement.

For Roger Dean, the meandering yet purposeful courses traced by pathways trodden by successive generations bespeak the mark of man in sympathy with his environment. Following them, we are impressed by their "rightness," apt as they are to the placing of water and earth, rock and tree, and also to our own mental processes. For Dean they symbolize a feeling, which though we may recognise it, we are as yet unable to sustain; the sense that we do know how to live in the world, that we are at home here.

It has been ten years since VIEWS was first published and the brothers Roger and Martyn Dean have been very busy in that time working on a range of projects from publishing, rock and roll stages and album covers to large architectural schemes. All this work is contained in the book MAGNETIC STORM the successor to VIEWS.

List of principal pictures

These are working titles of some of the principal pictures in this book and have only been used for convenience.

pages		Height in inches	Width in inches	G Gouache	E Enamel	W Watercolour	I Ink	M Montage	C Crayon
24	Gun	13	13	G		W	1		C
25	Green Dragon	16	16			W	1		
27-28	Black Plane	21	31		E		1	M	
33-34	Lighthouse	13	25	G	E	W			
38	Scarab	21	31		E		1	M	
39-40	Scarab	21	31		E		1	M	
43-44	Stage	28	36			W	1	M	
47-48	Octopus	31	42		E		1	M	
49	Skeleton	13	13	G			1		
51-52	Osibisa	13	25	G		W	1	M	
54	Osibisa Woyaya	13	25	G	E	W	1	M	
56	Del	13	13			W	1	M	
57	Budgie	17	14		E		1	M	
65-66	Paladin	24	42	G	E		1	M	
67	Nitro Function	13	16	G	E		1	M	
69-70	Wizard	31	42	G	E	W	1	M	C
71-72	Magician's Birthday	21	42			W	1	M	
73	Vertigo	30	30	G	E		1	M	
75-76	Spring	15	30			W	1		
79	Dragon's Dream	17	17		E		1		
83-84	Blue Demon	30	42	G	E		1	M	
89-90	Greenslade	21	41	G	E	W	1	M	
91-92	Greenslade and cats	13	25		E	W	1	M	
95-96	Badger	16	32			W			
101-102	Close to the Edge	13	25		E	W	1		
107-108	Yessongs—escape	24	31	G	E				
109-110	Yessongs—arrival	13	26			W	1		
111-112	Yessongs—awakening	13	26			W	1		
113-114	Yessongs—pathways	31	43	G		W	1		
117-118	Topographic Oceans	18	29	G		W	1		
119	Yesterdays—2 children	31	43	G	E	W	1	M	
120	Yesterdays—tree	13	13		E	W		M	
123-124	Relayer	16	32			W	1		
140	Green Castle	31	21	G	E		1	M	
145-146	Dragon and tree	13	25			W	1		
147-150	Dragon and village	14	42			W	1		
153-154	Steve Howe	16	32			W	1	M	